DIESTERWEGS
NEUSPRACHLICHE
BIBLIOTHEK

Ray Bradbury

There Will Come Soft Rains

Study Guide

by
Ingrid Stritzelberger

DIESTERWEG

NEUSPRACHLICHE BIBLIOTHEK

Ray Bradbury
There Will Come Soft Rains

Study Guide
by Ingrid Stritzelberger

Acknowledgements:
I'd like to thank my students for trying out my ideas with me, my family for their patience and the occasional photo, and Jenny Poole for keeping my British English up to par.
Big thanks go to our friend Cyrus Wairagu Maina who explained the Kenyan principle of celebrating life to me.

There's rosemary, that's for remembrance. Pray you, love, remember.
(Ophelia, in William Shakespeare's ***Hamlet***)

Druck A [1] / Jahr 2013
Alle Drucke der Serie A sind im Unterricht parallel verwendbar.

Redaktion: Ingrid Stritzelberger, Denkendorf
Herstellung: Harald Thumser, Frankfurt am Main
Satz: Stahringer Satz GmbH, Grünberg
Druck und Bindung: westermann druck GmbH, Braunschweig

ISBN 978-3-425-**09404**-8

Table of Contents

Introduction 4

How to Deal with the Topic 6

Pre-reading Activities

Dreams 8
Carpe Diem, *Dead Poets Society* (Film) 9
Life and Death 11

The short story and the poems in context 14

While-reading Activities I–IV

I Memento Mori
Introducing Death 16
Four Weddings and A Funeral (Film) 17
W. H. Auden: *Stop all the Clocks* 18
Bells 20
When I die 21
Time 22

II Nature/Mankind/Technology
Then, Now, in the Future 23

Ray Bradbury:
August 2026: There Will Come Soft Rains 24
Questions 26
Answers 28
Another House – The House of Usher 32
Yet Another Place 33

Survival
Duck and Cover 34
Survival Skills 35
Doomsday Preppers 38
Zombie Apocalypse 41
Emergency Plans 42
Secret Tests 44
E. M. Forster: *The Machine Stops* 45

III Response to Tragedy
Writing poems 47
The Sick Rose 48
The Icarus myth 49
W. H. Auden: *Musée des Beaux Arts* 50
Death and the Artist 52

IV Letting Go or Holding Tight
Quotes 54
Time Eternal 56
The Afterlife 57
The Right to Die 59
Gambling with DEATH 61
From Beyond the Grave 64
Keeping Memories Alive 65

Answers to Questions of Consideration 67

How to Continue 71

Post-reading Activities

Creative Obituary Projects 72
A 'Must-Read' Obituary 73
Obituary Writing 74
Remembering Roger Ebert 76

Test 77

Inspirational Thoughts 79

Introduction

Mourning death or celebrating life – these are the topics of this study guide and the students' books.

The purpose of this guide is two-fold. It is to show ways of dealing with the ample material in the students' book, and on the other hand it offers a multitude of worksheets which can be used directly in class. Students and teachers can profit from this material that has been tried out in the classroom.

There are many ways of approaching the topic of suffering, death and our ways of dealing with loss, our attitudes towards the living and the dead; and our society's approach to dealing with tragedies and mortality.

The following will first offer a summarised suggestion of how to deal with the material in the students' book, then some approaches for the material in the study guide, which, of course, can be intermingled, elaborated on or shortened in many places.

The introduction to the **students' book** (pp. 4–6) spells out many points to consider, not the least being that in our society, death is still one of the taboo topics. Living and dying is universal, though.

Dealing with the texts in the students' book, we see attitudes of overwhelming grief, uncaring watching, standing by and looking on, we see responsibility and guilt. Within that framework the role of technological progress and the advancement of mankind can be explored. It is fruitful for the work in class to summarise the texts on dystopianism (pp. 7–11), *The Old Masters of the Renaissance* (pp. 45–46), *The Story of Daedalus and Icarus* (pp. 40–42), as well as the biographies of Ray Bradbury (pp. 12–13) and W. H. Auden (pp. 47–48), including *A Note to Auden* (pp. 49–53).

A group of students should be responsible for preparing a written summary which will then be handed out to the class. The same approach might be taken with the Questions for Consideration. They must be answered by all; for each topic, one group is responsible to type the answers and hand them out to all. Suggested answers can be found in the Study Guide, on pages 66–69.

The material and teaching suggestions in this **study guide** are intended to provide considerable student interaction. Suggestions for listening and viewing tasks are given, for which transcripts are provided. Mortality in all its shades can be considered and discussed.

Our students have dreams. They envisage their future. They ask themselves what life is about.

In the pre-reading phase we can deal with these questions. Students should be asked to bring photographs of their parents or grandparents. With the help of these old photographs they can write stories about dreams these people might have had (p. 8). This should lead to a discussion of the concept of *Carpe Diem* – Seize the Day – with extracts from the film *Dead Poets Society* (pp. 9–10).

The while-reading material can be divided and dealt with in four phases:

The first phase can be named Memento Mori and includes Auden's poem ***Stop all the Clocks***. It deals with grief about dying, but also with seeing a purpose in life ending.

The second phase focuses on nature, mankind and technology and their interdependence. It includes Ray Bradbury's short story ***2026: There Will Come Soft Rains*** and Sara Teasdale's poem, which provides its title.

In the third phase, responses to tragedies will be considered with Auden's poem ***Musée des Beaux Arts*** and other material.

The fourth phase connects all the above. It reflects life, mortality and eternity by dealing with the concepts of letting go or holding tight.

In the post-reading phase, obituaries – their function and their content – are looked at. Morbid as it sounds, students are encouraged to think about what they would like to be remembered for. A look at inspirational quotes and their function will end this unit.

Picture references:

p. 8: Reinhold Mezger, Denkendorf
pp. 12, 13, 64, 65, 66, 80: Ingrid Stritzelberger, Denkendorf
p. 16: LEEMAGE/image.de
p. 17: Interfoto/Mary Evans
p. 22: Artothek/Museum of Modern Art, New York/© Salvador Dalí, Fundació Gala-Salvador Dalí/VG Bild-Kunst, Bonn 2013
p. 23 l: Interfoto/Mary Evans/Mary Evans Picture Library/John Maclellan
p. 23 r: fotolia.com/Bruce Shippee
p. 23 u: Kingly Properties, Las Vegas
p. 34: wikipedia.org
p. 40: www.amazon.com
p. 52: akg-images GmbH, Berlin/ARS Artists Rights Society, New York © 2013

How to Deal with the Topic

Dreams and loss, joy and death are contrasts – and pairs. In our work in the classroom, we can use the ideas of *Memento Mori* and *Carpe Diem* to introduce the students to the theory that our lives are comprised in these philosophies.

By showing selected scenes from *Dead Poets Society* (USA 1989, 128 min.) we can make them acquainted with these concepts. If the students themselves choose old pictures of their family or of people they know, they can write and talk about these people's dreams and if they came true. If the photo on page 8 is used, they can pick a person and speculate about their lives and dreams.

The analysis of the poem *Gather ye rosebuds while ye may* (Robert Herrick, 1591–1674), which can be presented as a drawing (p. 10), enforces the idea of the transience of life. More poems in the same vein can be included (pp. 11–12).

The drawing *All is Vanity* by Charles Allan Gilbert (p. 16) shows life and death interlaced and interdependent and gives room for discussion. This impetus can be used for the interpretation of Salvador Dali's painting *The Persistence of Memory* (p. 22).

In order to prepare the class for W. H. Auden's poem *Stop All the Clocks,* excerpts from the film *Four Weddings and a Funeral* (Britain 1994, 117 min.) can be used. We see Matthew's profound grief when he recites the poem at his partner Gareth's funeral (p. 17). His world has been deeply shaken and he believes every line he utters. After analysing the poem, the class should be encouraged to write a letter to Matthew.

Edgar Allan Poe's poem *The Bells*, of which an extract can be found on page 20, shows how closely joy and merriment are linked to death. Whereas this poem taints dying and death with frightening and menacing gloom, Philip Gould's thoughts *When I die* paint a different picture. He says that "My life became death. It gained a kind of quality and power as it never had before". The impressive video, which was recorded only weeks before his death, can be used for homework tasks and work in the classroom (p. 21).

A discussion on William Shakespeare's attitudes towards life and death can be started with the extracts on page 22. Students should present their ideas and express whether the extracts emphasise the futility of life or rather encourage the enjoyment of the here and now. The students should also state their own opinions.

Imminent death by a nuclear strike was a foremost fear in the Cold War period. When the prolific short story writer Ray Bradbury published *August 2026: There Will Come Soft Rains* in 1950, the nuclear attacks on Hiroshima and Nagasaki were very present in people's memories. The folly of thoughtless technological advancement and progress is the topic of this short story which is part of Ray Bradbury's *Martian Chronicles* – which, by the way, end with the human family abdicating earth standards and adopting Martian life.

Sara Teasdale's poem *There Will Come Soft Rains* should be analysed separately to show how Ray Bradbury uses her attitude that nature will conquer back a place destroyed by wars. Closer analysis shows that Ray Bradbury, in his story, does not present strong animals – the dog he introduces is covered in sores and dies, the foxes around the house are lonely, the cats whining. Radiation has weakened them. There are none of the happy nature sounds we find in Sara Teasdale's poem. The healing powers of soft rains are needed to turn destruction into an earthly paradise. This is yet to come.

Doing the tasks on the worksheets on pp. 26–27 the students can understand Ray Bradbury's preoccupation with technological progress and its dehumanising effects. To gain an insight into the anxieties of this period in post-war America, the students should view the short film *Duck and Cover* and discuss the material which advised the general public how to survive a catastrophe (pp. 34–37). The emergency plans of 2012 and the activities of the Doomsday Preppers can be compared with German material and approaches to emergencies (pp. 41–43).

Extracts from E.M. Forster's short story *The Machine Stops* (1909) should be contrasted with Ray Bradbury's presentation and interpretation of modern technology in *August 2026: There Will Come Soft Rains*. In E.M. Forster's story, a machine which was created by humans has then gained the mastery of their world. It provides for and rules over very passive human beings who live in underground cells because the world above ground is polluted. They hate human touch and communicate via internet-like media. They revere the machine like a god and treat the machine's handbook as a bible. Those who think differently are threatened with expulsion which is considered sure death. When the machine starts failing, people first complain but by and by accept its inadequacies. The machine's final collapse kills the underground population – but there is hope: some of those who were expelled survived and started a civilisation above ground.

After these stories on death caused by advanced technologies and how writers present these worlds, the focus should change and concentrate on spectators' perceptions and reactions on death. Students should summarise their ideas of death in eleven-word poems (p. 47). Before the Icarus myth is introduced, they should imagine situations in which a child dies, and possible reactions to this tragic event.

In W.H. Auden's poem *Musée des Beaux Arts*, we find the poet's interpretation of two paintings which he saw in Brussels. He states that the Old Masters presented the world as it is. An event, which can be life changing, like the birth of Jesus Christ, or tragic, like Icarus' fall into the sea, might be important to the nearest and dearest, but go unnoticed and unheeded by all others. Students should discuss what the author wants to express by showing the onlookers' indifference and disinterest and compare his poem with William Carlos Williams' *Landscape With The Fall of Icarus* (students' book, pp. 57–58).

The response to tragedy and death should be further dealt with under the heading Letting Go or Holding Tight. In this part students discuss quotes (pp. 54–55) and if they would grant a person the right to die (p. 59). Terry Pratchett's character Granny Weatherwax overcomes death in a game (pp. 61–63) and gives the topic a happier note. Knowing however, that Pratchett plans to commit suicide if his illness further incapacitates him gives food for thought.

Do near-death experiences show a glimpse of the afterworld? Are the pictures perceived just images fabricated by an overwrought brain? Or do they express the hope that death will not end all? Find out more and discuss the texts on pages 57 to 58.

Which ways of keeping awake memories of a beloved person do we consider appropriate – a memorial tribute on their death day in the paper? An interactive tombstone? Laying down wreaths? (p. 56; pp. 64–66) Whichever we decide on, we realise that students can profit from writing obituaries. They collect material and present it so that the person can be recognised and appreciated. They can also point out what they would like to be remembered for.

This guide and this unit end with a test and inspirational thoughts.

Pre-reading Activities

Worksheet Dreams

Tasks:

1. With your neighbour, talk about the people in the photo and give reasons why you prefer a certain one.
2. Write a story in which one person in the picture thinks and dreams of their future.

Class excursion in 1941

3. Bring photos of your family. Tell the others about the people in the pictures and if their dreams came true.

Pre-reading Activities

Worksheet *Carpe Diem*

Tasks:

1. Watch the first film sequence and write down what is important to the principal of Welton Academy.
2. What does the new teacher point out about education and life in the second sequence?
3. In order to explain the meaning of the poem in Extract 2, draw a small sketch.
4. Contrast the concepts of a successful and a happy life, as presented in the extracts.

Extract 1: Headmaster Nolan's Speech

Dead Poets Society, USA 1989, 128 min.

The gentleman with the candle walked to the front of the audience where the youngest students sat holding unlit candles. Slowly, he bent forward, lighting the candle of the first student on the aisle.

"The light of knowledge shall be passed from old to young," Headmaster Nolan intoned solemnly, as each boy lit the candle of the student sitting next to him.

"Ladies and gentlemen, distinguished alumni and students ... This year, 1959, marks the hundredth year that Welton Academy has been in existence. One hundred years ago, in 1859, forty-one boys sat in this room and were asked the same question that now greets you at the start of each semester." Nolan paused dramatically, his gaze sweeping the room full of intense, frightened young faces.

"Gentlemen," he bellowed, "what are the four pillars?"
The boys shouted in unison, "Tradition! Honor! Discipline! Excellence!"
Nolan nodded and the boys sat down.

"In her first year," Dean Nolan bellowed into the microphone, "Welton Academy graduated five students." He paused. "Last year we graduated fifty-one students and over 75 percent of those went to Ivy League schools!"

A burst of applause filled the room.
"This kind of accomplishment is the result of fervent dedication to the principles taught here."

[Various honour students who have carried in the banners recite the school's definitions of tradition, honour, discipline and excellence, after which the headmaster closes his speech:]

"Gentlemen," Dean Nolan continued, "at Welton you will work harder than you have ever worked in your lives, and your reward will be the success that all of us expect of you."

Extract 2: Mr Keating's First Lesson

Dead Poets Society, USA 1989, 128 min.

> *"Gather ye rosebuds while ye may,*
> *Old Time is still a flying;*
> *And this same flower that smiles today,*
> *Tomorrow will be dying."*

He stopped. "'Gather ye rosebuds while ye may'", Keating repeated. "The Latin term for that sentiment is Carpe Diem. Does anyone know what that means?"
"Carpe Diem," Meeks, the Latin scholar, said. "Seize the day."
"Seize the day," Keating repeated. "Why does the poet write these lines?"
"Because he's in a hurry?" one student called out as the others snickered.

"No. No, No! It's because we're food for worms, lads!" Keating shouted. "Because we're only going to experience a limited number of springs, summers, and falls. One day, hard as it is to believe, each and every one of us is going to stop breathing, turn cold, and die!" He paused dramatically. "Stand up," he urged the students, "and peruse the faces of the boys who attended this school sixty or seventy years ago. Don't be timid: go look at them."

"They are not that different than any of you, are they? Hope in their eyes, just like yours. They believe themselves destined for wonderful things, just like many of you. Well, where are those smiles now, boys? What of the hope? Did most of them not wait until it was too late before making their lives into even one iota of what they were capable? In chasing the almighty deity of success, did they not squander their boyhood dreams? However, if you get very close, boys, you can hear them whisper. Go on. Hear it? Can you?"

The boys were quiet, some of them leaned hesitantly toward the photographs. "Carpe Diem," Keating whispered loudly. "Seize the day. Make your lives extraordinary."

* * *

For the teacher:

"Gather Ye Rosebuds While Ye may", Robert Herrick, 1591–1674

ad 3: Seize the Day

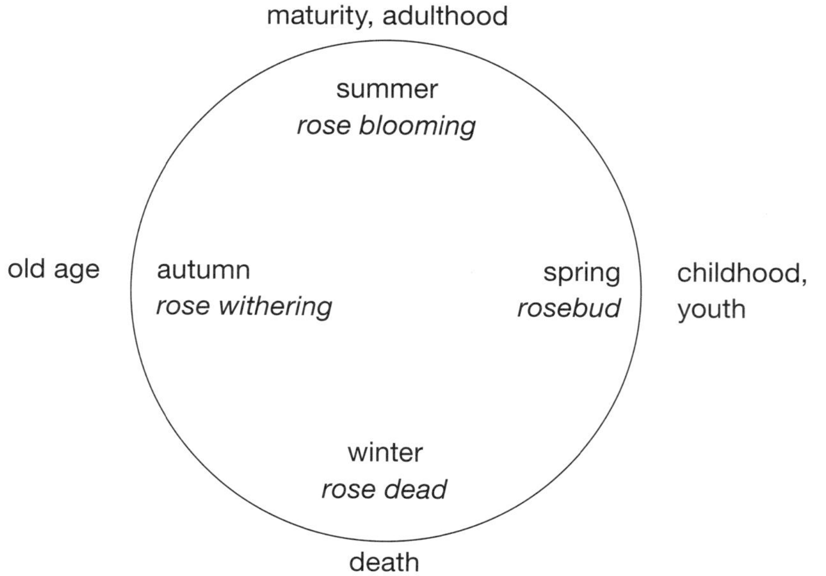

Pre-reading Activities

Worksheet Life and Death

Tasks:

1. Read the poem out loud. Concentrate on the last two paragraphs.
2. What atmosphere does the poem create?
3. What is the play called?
4. What does it mean that the hero of the play is the "Conqueror Worm"?
5. Compare the attitude towards men's role with Shakespeare's lines in the extract.
6. Read Jaques's monologue to compare Poe's and Shakespeare's attitudes towards life and death.

Poem: The Conqueror Worm

Edgar Allan Poe (1809–1849)

Lo! t'is a gala night
Within the lonesome latter years!
An angel throng, bewinged, bedight
In veils, and drowned in tears,
Sit in a theatre, to see
A play of hopes and fears,
While the orchestra breathes fitfully
The music of the spheres

Mimes, in the form of God on high,
Mutter and mumble low,
And hither and thither fly –
Mere puppets they, who come and go
At bidding of vast formless things
That shift the scenery to and fro,
Flapping from out their Condor wings
Invisible Woe!

That motley drama – oh, be sure
It shall not be forgot!
With its Phantom chased for evermore,
By a crowd that seize it not,
Through a circle that ever returneth in
To the self-same spot,
And much of Madness, and more of Sin,
And Horror the soul of the plot.

But see, amid the mimic rout
A crawling shape intrude!
A blood-red thing that writhes from out
The scenic solitude!
It writhes! – it writhes! – with mortal pangs
The mimes become its food,

And the angels sob at vermin fangs
        In human gore imbued.

Out – out are the lights – out all!
        And, over each quivering form,
The curtain, a funeral pall,
        Comes down with the rush of a storm,
And the angels, all pallid and wan,
        Uprising, unveiling, affirm
That the play is the tragedy "Man,"
        And its hero the Conqueror Worm.

Extract: **Merely Players**
William Shakespeare, from **As You Like It**, Act II, Scene 7

Jaques's monologue:

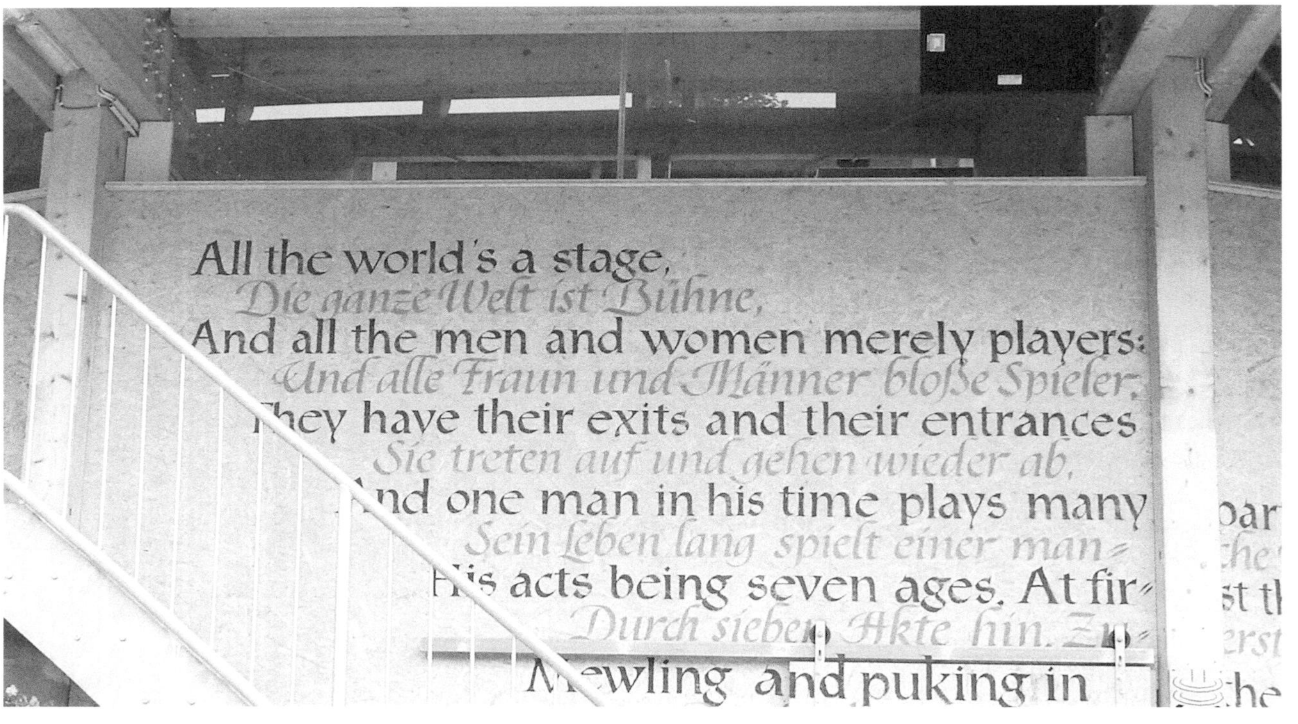

* * *

Further task:

In his monologue, Jaques mentions the seven roles in a person's life (infant, schoolboy, lover, soldier, judge, man in his dotage, senile and feeble man in his second childhood).

Either: Turn these stages into pictures or drawings. A flipbook works, too!

Or: Use matchsticks to represent human beings and to show the stages in a person's life.

Give your pictures or your work a title. Then present your pictures or your work to the class and explain what is most important for you.

For the teacher:

Poe's poem creates a gloomy, perhaps even frightening atmosphere.
Man's destiny, a tragedy of hopes and fears, madness, sins and horror, is unfolded as a play, in front of an audience of veiled angels in tears. The hero that finally enters the scene is a blood-red worm which devours the actors. When the lights go out and the curtain – a funeral pall – comes down, the angels take off their veils and deplore Man's fate.

Devouring worms are shown to be more powerful than human beings. They are a personification of death. All dreams come to nothing, humans are handled like puppets on a string and they will die without leaving a trace of their existence.

William Shakespeare points out the stages in the life of a human being, but emphasises the fact, too, that people are like puppets, not acting of their own free will.

Using matchsticks to represent human beings, the photo below shows five stages of a person's life: being born as a helpless little being, a crawling infant, a child, an adult, a weakening old person, a burnt-out, lifeless corpse. In this representation, humans appear, live their lives and disappear. No traces of their existence will be found when their lives are over.

So the idea of *Memento Mori*, remember that you will die, appeals very strongly in connection with the concept of *Carpe Diem*, seize the day, and creates the imperative: Make your life meaningful.

The short story and the poems in context

This overview serves as a quick reference as to which material is offered for the while-reading phases and under which headings the texts and worksheets can be dealt with. Depending on class situations, personal preferences and time available, topics can be shortened, their order can be interchanged, and tasks can be handed out as group tasks or homework assignments.

While-reading Activities I: Memento Mori

The concepts of *Memento Mori* and *Carpe Diem* have already been introduced in the pre-reading phase and can now be profoundly explored using

- the *Vanitas* painting by Charles Allan Gilbert, which represents a skull and a beautiful woman at her dressing table (also called vanity table) at the same time
- the film *Four Weddings and A Funeral* which includes W.H. Auden's poem *Stop All the Clocks*
- Poe's poem *The Bells* which paints a gloomy picture of a world ruled by ghouls
- a short video documentary in which Labour peer Philip Gould speaks about the death zone and about the lessons he has been learning in these last weeks of his life
- Dali's painting *The Persistence of Time*, in which time does not persist but disappears into all kinds of shapes and slips away
- quotations from Shakespeare plays about time passing and about death being the final and just leveller
- the poems *Night Funeral in Harlem* by Langston Hughes (students' book pp. 63–66) and *Alabanza: In Praise of Local 100* by Martin Espada (students' book, pp. 67–69). They offer a warm and caring view.

It might be interesting to divide the class into four groups and to allocate one poem from the *Memento Mori* section to each group. They prepare their arguments in their groups and then defend and uphold the views of the poet in a subsequent class discussion. The groups can then agree which poem they want to turn into a short film, a PowerPoint presentation, an audio recording or a live presentation on stage.

While-reading Activities II: Nature-Mankind-Technology

This part is two-fold. It introduces the idea of technological progress and its benefits but also its dangers. Can and will mankind survive? The second part deals with surviving man-made catastrophes and presents the gloomy science fiction story *The Machine Stops*, in which the failure of the Machine also kills the humans relying on it. Only a few who have been expelled from this perfect technological world to live like savages above ground survive the final catastrophe. The fact that survival is not just a topic of the Cold War period is pointed out with more modern material, for example the 2013 TV series *Doomsday Preppers* broadcast by the National Geographic Channel.

The material on progress comprises

- photos of kitchens in 1920, 1970 and in 2010
- a summary of Ray Bradbury's short story *August 2026: There Will Come Soft Rains*
- Ray Bradbury's short story *August 2026: There Will Come Soft Rains* (students' book, pp. 14–22)
- worksheets with tables and questions for students about the story
- answers and hints for the teacher with a closer look at Sara Teasdale's poem
- Poe's *The Fall of the House of Usher,* a house that has a life of its own and, by imprinting its character (and feelings) onto its inhabitants, spreads its gloomy and deadly influence on the once-mighty Ushers
- *The Ballad of the Haunted Palace,* part of the above-mentioned short story. Like Sara Teasdale's poem in Ray Bradbury's story, this ballad is a short summing up of the perdition and destruction of the House of Usher.
- a ghost city which is totally automated to run tests for a fully mechanised world with self-driving cars, "intelligent" houses and further smart technology

Survival in a world controlled by technology and shaken by nuclear fears is presented with

- *Duck and Cover (1951),* a film shown in schools as part of a civil protection programme. Turtle Bert teaches how to duck and cover as a first-response action to nuclear attacks, and where to find shelter.
- Manuals on *Self-help Civil Defense*
- the 2013 television show *Doomsday Preppers*, which presents people who make it their task to be fully prepared for final catastrophes and rely on their own means to survive
- the Zombie Survival Kit which can be ordered from Amazon, to go with …
- … the 'Zombie apocalypse', as the Homeland Security Department luridly calls its campaign to encourage citizens to prepare for emergencies
- German governmental advice on preparing for catastrophes. The scenarios recommend providing for emergencies which could last for about two weeks, to bridge the period until official helpers such as firemen, etc., step in
- survivors of dangerous tests in St. Louis, who raise their concerns about being used as guinea pigs
- *The Machine Stops*, a 1909 science fiction story in which an underground world is dehumanised and ruled by a machine which becomes gradually defective and kills all who are dependent on it

While-reading Activities III: Response to Tragedy

Ways of dealing with tragedy can be explored using the following texts and suggestions:

- writing eleven-word-poems about death
- William Blake's poem *The Sick Rose*, which he includes in his cycle "Songs of Experience" showing that joy and death are closely connected and that feelings make us vulnerable but also human
- a child dying, making a drawing of the Icarus myth, reactions to other people's suffering
- comparing the drawing with Brueghel's paintings and W.H. Auden's poem *Musée des Beaux Arts,* as well as with William Carlos Williams' poem *Landscape with the Fall of Icarus*
- Should I be my brother's keeper? Introduction to the Old Testament verses about Cain and Abel followed by reading James Hurst's short story *The Scarlet Ibis.* It can be found in the students' book on pages 70–79.

While-reading Activities IV: Letting Go or Holding Tight

This part brings together all aspects about mortality and eternity, love and grief.
Students can discuss their attitudes with the following material:

- quotes presenting the concepts of "letting go and remembering" or of "holding on tightly in order not to forget"
- memorial tributes to loved ones on their death days
- grief and the hope of future happiness in John Dowland's poem *O what hath overwrought*
- a positive account of a glimpse at the afterlife
- a powerful appeal to be assisted in order to die a dignified death
- a literary extract about a Discworld witch fighting for a baby and gambling with DEATH. Many students are familiar with Terry Pratchett's novels. Perhaps they have also read or seen his talks about assisted death and know that he intends to end his life if his illness gets too debilitating.
- memories from beyond the grave with interactive tombstones
  This can be turned into a media task in which students produce and present how they want to be remembered and what makes them unique
- photos of war cemeteries, where memories from beyond the grave strike a nerve by their sheer mass

Answers to Questions of Consideration

In this part, the answers to the questions of consideration, which are presented in the students' books, are collected.

While-reading Activities I

Worksheet Memento Mori – Introducing Death

Tasks:

1. Rephrase this biblical quotation in your own words:
   Ecclesiastes: 12, 7–8 *Then shall the dust return to the earth as it was; and the spirit shall return unto God who gave it. Vanity of vanities, saith the preacher; all is vanity.*
   (King James Version)
2. Describe the picture below.
3. What does the artist wish to express?

Charles Allan Gilbert: *All is Vanity* (1895)

While-reading Activities I

Worksheet Memento Mori – *Four Weddings and A Funeral*

Tasks:

1. Describe the picture below. What do you expect to happen?
2. *The wedding*: Watch the film sequence and write down what we find out about Gareth at Carrie's and Hamish's wedding in Scotland.
3. *The funeral*: Watch the film sequence. What does Matthew add about Gareth in his eulogy?
4. How does he recite the poem "Stop all the clocks" and how are we affected by it?
5. Find out more about Matthew's situation at the end of the film. Comment, also refer to the poem.

Four Weddings and A Funeral (Britain 1994, 117 min.)

Gareth (middle) and Matthew (right)

For the teacher:

ad 5:

Though sincerely broken-hearted at Gareth's funeral – when he recites the poem showing his feelings for his partner –, we see Matthew with a new boyfriend at the end of the film. Time seems to have healed his wounds.

Worksheet Memento Mori – Stop all the Clocks

Tasks:

1. Refer to the poem with annotations in the students' book, pp. 60–62.
2. What situation is the writer of the poem in?
3. Collect the positive attributes of "Him" and what He means to the writer.
4. a) How should grief be shown? Make a list.
   b) Comment on what the writer demands.
5. What does the writer of the poem expect for his future?
6. As a friend, write a letter to him.

Poem: Stop all the Clocks

W. H. Auden (1936; 1938/40)

Stop all the clocks, cut off the telephone,
Prevent the dog from barking with a juicy bone,
Silence the pianos and with muffled drum
Bring out the coffin, let the mourners come.

Let aeroplanes circle moaning overhead
Scribbling on the sky the message He Is Dead
Put crepe bows round the white necks of the public doves,
Let the traffic policemen wear black cotton gloves.

He was my North, my South, my East and West,
My working week and my Sunday rest,
My noon, my midnight, my talk, my song,
I thought that love would last for ever. I was wrong.

The stars are not wanted now: put out every one;
Pack up the moon and dismantle the sun;
Pour away the ocean and sweep up the wood.
For nothing now can ever come to any good.

For the teacher:

ad 2:

These thoughts are expressed in a situation of inconsolable grief, of deep mourning, perhaps at a burial service, on the cemetery, while thinking of a beloved person. Perhaps the coffin will soon be carried out and lowered into the ground.

In the nineteenth century, clocks were stopped and mirrors veiled while a wake was held in the house. The custom of not ringing bells between Good Friday and Easter, but using ratchets instead, can still be observed in traditional Roman Catholic communities in Austria and Switzerland.

ad 3:

He is dead.

He was ...

– North/South/East/West	= geographic directions	denoting the whole world
– working week/Sunday rest	= temporal references	denoting all the time
– noon/midnight	= light + dark	denoting all moods
– talk, song	= means of communication	denoting connection to the world around

He is vitally important to the writer because he is his whole world, fills all his time, embraces him in all his moods and is his link to the world around him. He provides the writer's personal well-being and protects his whole existence.

ad 4:

All ordinary actions should be stopped, the celestial bodies should be dismantled, the world should be put away and the oceans emptied.

These unrealistic demands cannot and will not be met. The moon cannot be packed up nor all telephones silenced. Doves will not wear black crepe bows nor will policemen don black gloves. The clocks cannot be stopped. Time will go on.

ad 5:

The mourner does not expect any positive future. There is no light anymore, for him everything has died. He is full of melancholy and sadness.

ad 6:

Individual answers.

In this context there is no need to mention that the 1936 version of *Stop All the Clocks* or *Funeral Blues* was a satiric poem of mourning for a political leader. This poem ends with a fifth stanza:

> And Gunn, of course, will drive a motor-hearse;
> None could drive it better, most would drive it worse.
> He'll open up the throttle to its fullest power
> And drive him to the grave at ninety miles an hour.

While-reading Activities I

Worksheet Memento Mori – Bells

Tasks:

1. With your neighbour, find as many situations as possible connected with bells. Make a list and present them to the class.
2. Read the extract from the poem "The Bells" and point out which events are announced by the bells. Are there more or less on your list?
3. Media task: Record bells and make the others find out what their ringing means.
4. Read the whole poem to find out who tolls the bells. Which effect does this poem achieve?
5. Leonard Cohen has a different approach. Present his song "Anthem" (2009) and explain the song and its chorus (Extract 2).

Extract 1: The Bells

Edgar Allan Poe (1809–1849)

I
Hear the sledges with the bells –
    Silver bells!
What a word of merriment their melody foretells! …
II
Hear the mellow wedding bells,
    Golden bells!
What a world of happiness their harmony foretells! …
III
Hear the loud alarum bells –
    Brazen bells!
What a tale of terror, now, their turbulency tells! …
IV
Hear the tolling of the bells –
    Iron bells!
What a world of solemn thought their melody compels!
    In the silence of the night,
    How we shiver with affright
At the melancholy menace of their tone! …

Extract 2: Anthem

Leonard Cohen, 2009

Ring the bells that still can ring
Forget your perfect offering
There is a crack in everything
That's how the light gets in.

While-reading Activities I

Worksheet Memento Mori – When I die

Tasks:

1. Watch the video *When I die*, in which Philip Gould shares his thoughts about his impending death www.youtube.com/watch?v=S2eUw0CUuMc and take notes.
2. How does he see this period in his life? Quote and explain.
3. Write a message to a friend about this video.
4. Discuss this video and relate it to this quotation: "I think death is a tremendous adventure – a gateway into a new life, in which you have further powers, deeper joys, and wonderful horizons." (Dr. Leslie D. Weatherhead)

Extract from the Video: When I Die: Lessons from the Death Zone

released 19 April 2012, Director and Photographer: Adrian Steirn (8.51 min.)

Philip Gould: In six weeks' time, I will be dead. I will be cremated. I will face huge fare but it is an extra-ordinary experience.

This is the most exciting and the most extraordinary journey of my life. My only regret is it ends. I'd like to be on this journey with you almost forever and a day.

It's only when they say, y'know, Philip Gould, you are going to die, get used to it and this is going to happen in weeks or months, it is only when that happens you're aware of death. And only when that happens also then suddenly life screams at you in its intensity.

I saw my children born, I saw them born and it showed the massive incredible intensive potential of that moment. And when my father died and the air left his body it was as powerful as the air entering the body of my daughters.

And I knew that the purpose here now was to give as much love as I could to people who mattered to me, even though I was dying. And my life became death. It gained a kind of quality and a power as it never had before. It entered a new zone which was the death zone.

* * *

Further task:

Watch the documentary *Terry Pratchett: Choosing To Die* (2011), in which he discusses his illness (he suffers from Alzheimer's) and his decision to end his life.
http://www.youtube.com/watch?v=slZnfC-V1SY

To the teacher:

In his last weeks before he died from oesophageal cancer Labour peer and strategist Philip Gould was filmed talking about his life and death. He explains his search for meaning and purpose of life "in the death zone".

While-reading Activities I

Worksheet Memento Mori – Time

Tasks:

1. Describe the picture below.
2. What does the artist wish to show?
3. How does Shakespeare express the futility of life? Refer to the extracts below. Do they express what you think?

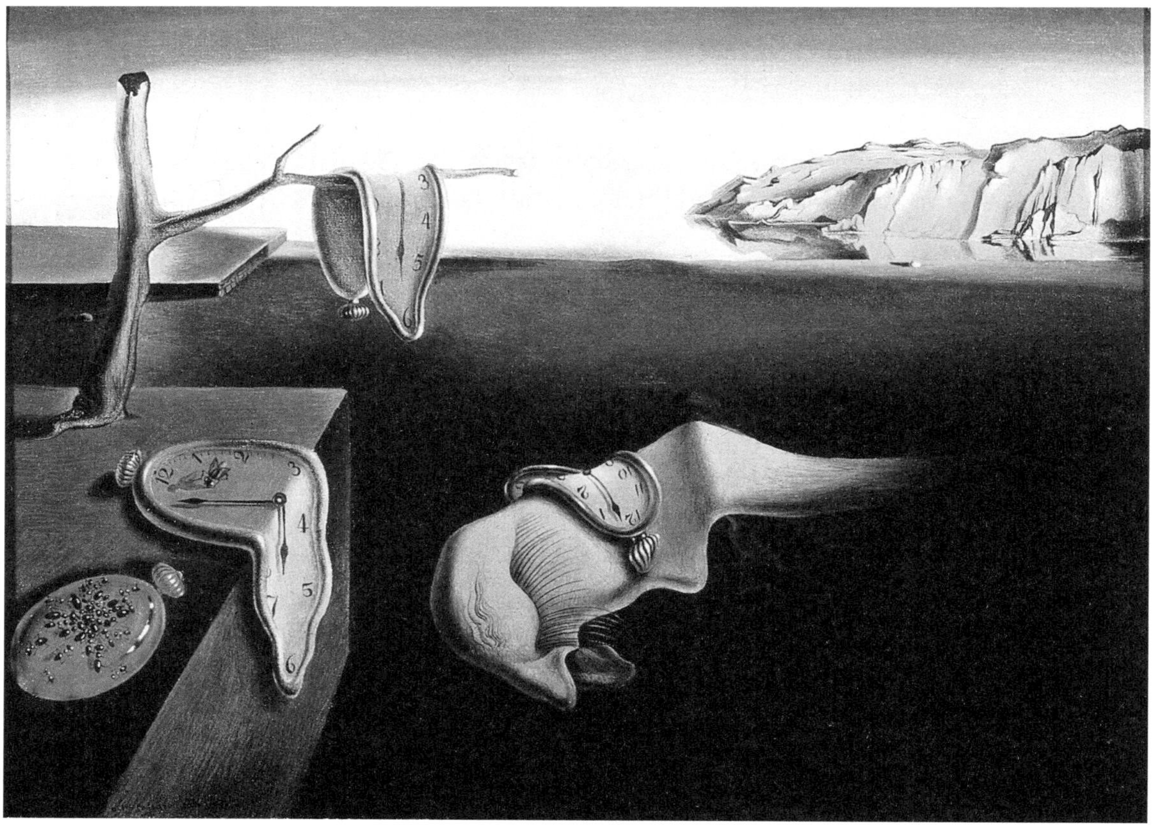

Salvador Dali, *The Persistence of Memory*, 1931

Extract 1: Fear no more
William Shakespeare,
Cymbeline, Act 4, Sc. 2

Fear no more the heat o' the sun,
nor the furious winter's rages.
Thou thy worldly task hast done,
home art gone, and ta'en thy wages.
Golden lads and girls all must,
as chimney sweepers, come to dust.

Extract 2: Thereby hangs a tale
William Shakespeare,
As You Like It, Act 2, Sc. 7

'It is ten o'clock:
Thus we may see,' quoth he, 'how the world wags:
'Tis but an hour ago since it was nine,
And after one hour more' twill be eleven;
And so, from hour to hour, we ripe and ripe,
And then, from hour to hour, we rot and rot;
And thereby hangs a tale.'

While-reading Activities II

Worksheet Nature/Mankind/Technology – Then, Now, in the Future

Tasks:

1. Compare the pictures of households. Jot down a few ideas about the life of the people who work in these kitchens.
2. Work in pairs. Make a list of the electronic household and entertainment equipment you have in your homes. Compare your two lists and agree on three items which are most important to you. Present them to the others.
3. Make a little drawing of how you imagine a kitchen to look in 2026.

Photos

Kitchen 1920

Kitchen 2010

Kitchen 1970
This kitchen is part of an underground home. Avon magnate Jerry Henderson had the bunker built in Las Vegas in 1970 as a bulwark against World War III.

August 2026: There Will Come Soft Rains

When Ray Bradbury wrote this short story in 1950, the Second World War had barely ended. The Korean War had started and found Russian and American forces fighting a proxy war. A palpable fear of nuclear strikes was evident. People worried about mankind's chances of surviving and wondered whether the advancements in technological progress would prove to be humanity's downfall.

This is the context of *August 2026: There Will Come Soft Rains* which starts with the seemingly idyllic description "In the living room the voice-clock sang, *Tick-tock, seven o'clock, time to get up, time to get up, seven o'clock!*" to be parried by the sentence "The morning house lay empty". Breakfast is prepared and served, for two adults and two children, judging from the eight slices of toast, two cups of coffee and two glasses of milk. Further announcements remind the family of payment dates for insurance and further bills, birthdays and anniversaries, and give a weather forecast.

It is raining on the empty house in which the garage doors open automatically to show a car which is not used, and in which the uneaten breakfast is scraped off the plates and washed down the sink. Robot cleaning mice bustle about and disappear again when the house is spotless.

The sun comes out when the rain stops. While this normally turns the world into a friendlier place, we are in for a shock when we are introduced to the surroundings of the house "The house stood alone in a city of rubble and ashes. This was the one house left standing. At night the ruined city gave off a radioactive glow which could be seen for miles."

A nuclear catastrophe destroyed the city around the house. Nevertheless, the electronic appliances of the house run through their pre-programmed schedules and the sprinklers water the lawn. A description of the west side wall reveals the inhabitants' fate. Etched into a blackened wall, five silhouettes can be seen: a man mowing the lawn, a woman picking flowers and a boy and a girl playing ball. The gentle sprinkler rain which falls on the garden is in stark contrast to the shapes of the burnt family.

When the lonely house starts protecting itself against stray animals we realise that not all life has perished. A sparrow touches the window shades, lonely foxes and mewling cats are driven away; the door, however, recognises the whine of the emaciated, haggard family dog. It is covered in sores and tries desperately to first find the family and then to get into the kitchen where the midday meal is being prepared. Mad with hunger and unable to scratch its way into the kitchen, it dies. The corpse is cleared away by the mice and burnt in the incinerator in the cellar.

The afternoon routine with a bridge party for the wife starts and ends. Then the children's room is prepared for their playtime. The walls start to glow and present an artificial reality: a field with iron crickets, jungle rains, exotic animals, strange sounds and smells.

Bath water is prepared, dinner is served, a fire is lit and a cigar is ready. The poem which is randomly chosen is "*There Will Come Soft Rains*". It expresses the hope that following human-made destruction nature will take over and repair the damage – Sara Teasdale's reaction to the atrocities of World War I.

The fire burns down, the music plays on and we expect the routine to continue, when we are startled out of our complacency by the next sentence "At ten o'clock the house began to die." It is nature that interferes and starts a chain of events: Heavy winds crash a bough into the kitchen; it breaks a bottle of cleaning solvent. The liquid spreads over the stove and sets the room ablaze. The house, which is equipped to fight fire, does not have sufficient reserves any more after all the useless lawn watering and bathing routines. The attack of the fire and the defence of the house are presented like a military campaign in which the fire, sneakier and more tenacious, gains the upper hand when it destroys the house's control centre in the attack.

One after the other, the electronic voices die, equipment and furniture burn, even the artificial jungle animals in the children's room get frightened and run off. In a final maniacal surge, announcements can be heard, the lawn is cut, doors open and shut, mice scurry back and forth, while poetry is read until the last circuits burst. A final effort of preparing food is made by the fully automated kitchen when the house collapses and stops all.

All but one circuit.
The next morning is sunny and reveals the ruins of the house with one wall still standing. And the last circuit announcing a new day "Today is August 5, 2026".

This new date shows that "life" will go on. Although signs of wildlife (sparrow, foxes) have been spotted earlier in the story, it will take a long time until nature can reclaim the polluted ground and ruined places. But as Sara Teasdale's poem probably was the one played by the poetry tape, we keep up our hopes and wait for the healing, gentle rains that wash away the after-effects of destruction and make room for a new beginning.

Worksheet Questions on *August 2026: There Will Come Soft Rains*

Tasks:

Before reading the story ***August 2026: There Will Come Soft Rains***, discuss with your neighbour what you expect from a story with this title. Present your ideas to the others.

I. While reading the story, fill in the timeline of what goes on and when on August 4, 2026.

When	What	Weather conditions
7.00 a.m.		
7.09		
8.01		
8.30		
9.15		
10.00		
10.15		
12.00		
2.00 p.m.		
2.15		
2.35		
4.00		
4.30		
5.00		
6.00		
7.00		
8.00		
9.00		
9.05		
10.00		
next day, dawn		

II. Colour code the story. Use one colour for man-made artefacts, another one for nature.

What becomes obvious in the course of the story?

III. Answer the following questions.

1. When and where is the story set?
2. For how many persons is breakfast being prepared?
3. Which announcements do the voices make?

4. Describe how the kitchen and the other rooms are being cleaned.
5. What is there surrounding the house?
6. Point out the contrasts in the description of the outside of the house.
7. Draw the west facade of the house. Or scratch it out of a wax-covered surface.
8. What must have happened?
9. Make a list of the animals around the house.
10. In which context is religion mentioned? Explain what is meant by gods.
11. Sum up what happens to the dog.
12. Which entertainment is provided for the afternoon? What does that say about the family's occupations?
13. Is there anything you think noteworthy about the evening routine?
14. After having a closer look at the poem, sort the words into the columns provided.

Sara Teasdale, *There Will Come Soft Rains* (1920)

Nature			Human beings	Man-made
weather + seasons	**plants + soil**	**animals + their sounds**		
soft rains				

15. What mood does the poem convey? What does Bradbury want to say with it?
16. Why are we shocked when we read the phrase "At ten o'clock the house began to die"?
17. In the next passages, colour code fire and fire-related expressions red, technological or man-made items blue, nature green, and death and destruction black. What do the paragraphs look like?
18. What starts the fire and why is it not extinguished by the water rats?
19. Underline the military terms used in connection with the fire and explain the strategy the fire uses to devour the house. Give examples to show the personification of fire.
20. How does the house react to the massive assault?
21. What is the last electronic device that goes bust? And the last machinery equipment?
22. What is left of the house?
23. Dawn appears despite total destruction. Refer to the poem. What is mentioned there? What does this mean?

IV. Divide the story into parts and give them titles or one-line summaries.

V. List ideas why Ray Bradbury wrote this story. Discuss them with your neighbour and present them to the class.

While-reading Activities II

August 2026: There Will Come Soft Rains Questions and Answers

For the teacher:

I. Timeline August 4, 2026

When	What	Weather
7.00 a.m.	"Tick-tock, seven o'clock, time to get up" – The speaking clock wakes the household.	rain
7.09	"seven-nine, breakfast time": Breakfast is being prepared.	
8.01	"eight-one, tick-tock, eight-one o'clock, off to school, off to work, run, run, eight-one" The garage door opens, stays open for a while, closes again.	
8.30	Shrivelled eggs and hard toast are scraped into the rubbish bin.	
9.15	"Nine-fifteen, time to clean". Robot mice clean the rooms.	
10.00	The sun comes out and shines on this house amidst the rubble.	sun
10.15	The garden sprinklers come on.	
12.00	An emaciated dog with sores is let into the house, finds no one. Tries to get to the food which the kitchen prepares. Dies. Lies in the parlour for an hour.	
2.00 p.m.	The mice clean up.	
2.15	The dog is burnt in the incinerator in the cellar.	
2.35	Bridge tables, playing cards, martinis, egg-salad sandwiches and music – all is set for a bridge party	
4.00	The party is over, tables disappear.	
4.30	Nursery wall glow for the children's hour.	
5.00	The bathtub is filled with hot water.	
6.00	Dinner is served.	
7.00	Dinner is cleared.	
8.00	There is a fire in the hearth, a cigar is lit.	
9.00	Beds are warmed.	
9.05	The poem *There Will Come Soft Rains* is being read.	
10.00	The destruction of the house begins when a fire starts.	storm, wind
next day, dawn	The house has collapsed. The electronic clock announces a new day.	sun

II. Colour code the story. Use one colour for man-made artefacts, another one for nature.

What becomes obvious in the course of the story?
- man-made artefacts disappear
- nature takes over and wins

III. Answer the following questions.

1. When and where is the story set?

It is set in Allendale, California on August 4, 2026. The house belongs to the McClellan family.

2. For how many persons is breakfast being prepared?
Breakfast is being prepared for four, presumably two adults who drink coffee and two children.

3. Which announcements do the voices make?
They announce the time and the weather. They remind the listener of birthdays and anniversaries and of payments that are due.

4. Describe how the kitchen and the other rooms are being cleaned.
The uneaten breakfast is scraped off the plates and washed down the sink, the dishes are cleaned in a washer. The rooms are being cleaned by mice-like robots made of rubber and metal.

5. What is there surrounding the house?
The empty house is surrounded by rubble and ashes. It is part of a city in ruins which was destroyed by a radioactive blast, by an atomic bomb.

6. Point out the contrasts in the description of the outside of the house.
The water of the garden sprinklers creates golden reflections; the air is soft, the sun comes out in patches of brightness. On the other hand, the west side of the house is charred and burned, the wall is black, save for five silhouettes: a man, a woman, a boy, a girl and a ball.

7. Draw the west facade of the house. Or scratch it out of a wax-covered surface.
- a man mowing the lawn
- a woman picking flowers
- a boy and girl playing ball

8. What must have happened?
In an atomic blast, the family was outdoors and burnt to cinders in seconds. Their presence protected the white paint on the wall from the fiery blast and "etched" their silhouettes on the otherwise burnt and black wall. The whole city around their house is in ruins, too. Only the machines keep working in their pre-programmed schedules.

9. Make a list of the animals that are around the house.
There are lonely foxes, stray cats, birds, for example sparrows.

10. In which context is religion mentioned? Explain what is meant by gods.
The house is described as an altar, the machines and robots are attending and servicing the religious service in choirs – in big groups. But because the gods have gone, the rituals are meaningless. There are no longer any people in the house – they used to be "the gods". The incinerator in the basement is compared to the heathen god Baal. There are no longer any references to Christian beliefs.

11. Sum up what happens to the dog.
The dirty, sick, emaciated dog is recognized by the automatic door opener and let into the house. There, it desperately searches for the family, then tries to get into the kitchen where a meal is being prepared. Mad with hunger, it collapses and dies. The "cleaning mice" clear the cadaver away. It is burnt in the incinerator in the basement.

12. Which entertainment is provided for the afternoon? What does that say about the family's occupations?
A game of bridge is provided for the mistress of the house and at least three friends. That seems to show that women did not work but just had fun (hedonistic society).
The children have artificial adventures – nursery walls glow, shapes of animals appear, the floor is turned into a meadow, nature sounds are heard. Playtime means being immersed in an articial world, for example a jungle. For indoor playing, a lot of artificial amusement is provided and obviously regularly used.

13. Is there anything you think noteworthy about the evening routine?
It sounds like pleasurable routine: After the bath, all is quite calm, but cultured and comfortable: a fire in the fireplace, a cigar waiting for the husband, the beds being warmed and a poem being read out.

14. After having a closer look at the poem, sort the words into the columns provided.

Sara Teasdale, *There Will Come Soft Rains* (1920)

Nature			**Human beings**	**Man-made**
weather + seasons	**plants + soil**	**animals + their sounds**		
soft rains	smell of ground	swallows with shimmering sound	mankind	low fence-wire
night	wild plum trees	frogs singing	**we**	war
spring	tree	robins whistling		
dawn		bird		

15. What mood does the poem convey? What does Bradbury want to say with it?
Mankind is not needed by nature. Technology, which played such an important role in this highly technified world, destroyed mankind, its creators, in a war. -- But nature is not bothered, does not care. It goes on. After the destruction by humans, nature's soft rains have healing powers and turn the world into a natural paradise.

16. Why are we shocked when we read the phrase "At ten o'clock the house began to die"?
All the other times mention a daily recurrence, a routine. This one doesn't, it is a one-off – the mould is broken and destruction sets in.

17. In the next passages, colour code fire and fire-related expressions red, technological or man-made items blue, nature green, and death and destruction black. What do the paragraphs look like?
Nature gradually disappears. Fire and technology compete, until death and destruction prevail.

18. What starts the fire and why is it not extinguished by the water rats?
A storm wind crashes a nearby tree through the window, knocking a strong chemical down and onto the stove. This catches fire immediately. The reserve water supply, which has not been refilled, has used up all the water by washing dishes and having baths ready, so there is no more water for the water rats to use.

19. Underline the military terms used in connection with the fire and explain the strategy the fire uses to win. Give examples to show the personification of fire.
- reinforcements, to back off, explosion, (bronze) shrapnel, brave

The fire is being driven back by blind robots spouting green chemicals. But it uses a ruse (personification) and climbs up the outside walls of the house and destroys the pumps in the attic. Some mice are very brave and do their duty.

20. How does the house react to the massive assault?
It fights back with its last defences of technology – tapes are played, the grass is cut, etc.; "maniac confusion, yet unity" is described.

21. What is the last electronic device that goes bust? And the last machinery equipment?
The tape running a poem is the last to "die" – we assume that it plays the same poem as before, announcing soft rains. The stove prepares huge amounts of food, before it is engulfed by fire and the house collapses.

22. What is left of the house?
Only one wall is still standing with the mechanical and utterly pointless announcement of the date: "Today is August 5, 2026".

23. Dawn appears despite total destruction. Refer to the poem. What is mentioned there? What does this mean?

Dawn, as well as spring, which is mentioned in the poem, symbolises a new beginning. In the story, of all the man-made machinery, only the useless mechanical clock is left when the sun, a symbol of life, rises, and nature takes over.

IV. Divide the story into parts and give them titles or one-line summaries

	Pages/lines	Parts	Titles/one-line summaries
1	p. 14 – p. 15, l. 10	Description of the house and its surroundings	Introducing the house and its workings
2	p. 15, l. 10 – p. 16, l. 5		Destruction and death, rubble, and silhouettes of the family on the facade
3	p. 16, ll. 6–16		The lonely house protects itself from nature and animals.
4	p. 16, l. 17 – p. 17, l. 17		Dog arrives at lonely house, dies and is disposed of
5	p. 17, ll. 18–24	Daily routine	Daily routine continues: bridge party for housewife in the afternoon
6	p. 17, l. 25 – p. 18, l. 14		Virtual reality, hologram walls for children when they come home from school
7	p. 18, ll. 15–21		Bath for children, evening meal, bedtime
8	p. 18, l. 22 – p. 19, l. 3		Relaxing in front of the fireplace; the recital of Sara Teasdale's poem *There Will Come Soft Rains* starts
9	p. 19, ll. 4–18		The poem expresses the certitude that Spring (nature) will take over and offer a fresh start.
10	p. 19, l. 19 – p. 20, l. 4	Destruction	Wobbly tree crashes into kitchen, spilt solvent causes a fire
11	p. 20, ll. 5–14		No more water left after useless bathing and washing-up routine; fire spreads
12	p. 20, l. 15 – p. 21, l. 4		The house defends itself, but the fire attacks in a warlike campaign and finally burns the house down.
13	p. 21, l. 5 – p. 22, l. 11		The electric appliances die one after the other; the electronic voices become mute; poetry is still read.
14	p. 22, ll. 12–15		After explosions the house collapses.
15	p. 22, ll. 16–20	A new day = a fresh start	The electronic clock announces a new day; life goes on, without the house. Nature takes over.

V. List ideas why Ray Bradbury wrote this story. Discuss them with your neighbour and present them to the class.

Ray Bradbury, who belongs to the group of writers of dystopian literature, expresses his preoccupation with man-made technology and man-made weapons that do not advance mankind but annihilate it. That is why he chose Sara Teasdale's poem, which she wrote after WW I, to name and illustrate this short story, and to show his fears. WW II ended with the US dropping nuclear bombs on Hiroshima and Nagasaki, and at the time of his writing the short story, Russian and American troops faced each other in Korea.

While-reading Activities II

Worksheet Nature/Mankind/Technology – Another House

Tasks:

1. From the introductory passage in Extract 1, what do you expect to encounter in the short story?
2. How does the inset poem deal with time (the past, the present and the future)?
3. Compare the houses in this story and in Ray Bradbury's story. Use the quotation from Poe's story in which Roderick Usher believes in "the sentience of all vegetable things", "the evidence of the sentience was to be seen in that silent yet importunate and terrible influence (of the house) which for centuries had moulded the destinies of his family".

Extract 1: The House

Edgar Allan Poe, ***The Fall of the House of Usher*** (1839)

During the whole of a dull, dark, and soundless day in the autumn of the year, when the clouds hung oppressively low in the heavens, I had been passing alone, on horseback, through a singularly dreary tract of country, and at length found myself, as the shades of the evening drew on, within the view of the melancholy House of Usher. I know not how it was – but, with the first glimpse of the building, a sense of insufferable gloom pervaded my spirit. I looked upon the scene before me – upon the mere house, and the simple landscape features of the domain – upon the bleak walls – upon the vacant eye-like windows – upon a few white trunks of decayed trees – with an utter depression of soul which I can compare to no earthly sensation more properly than to the after-dream of the reveller upon opium – the bitter lapse into everyday life – the hideous dropping of the veil. There was an iciness, a sinking, a sickening of the heart – an unredeemed dreariness of thought which no goading of the imagination could torture into aught of the sublime. What was it – I paused to think – what was it that so unnerved me in the contemplation of the House of Usher? It was a mystery all insoluble.

Extract 2: The Ballad of "The Haunted Palace"

It consists of 6 stanzas and is part of the story ***The Fall of the House of Usher***.

I. In the greenest of our valleys,
  By good angels tenanted,
Once a fair and stately palace –
  Radiant palace – reared its head.
In the monarch Thought's dominion –
  It stood there! […]
II. Banners yellow, glorious, golden
  On its roof did float and flow
(This – all this – was in the olden
  Time long ago) […]
V. But evil things, in robes of sorrow,
  Assailed the monarch's high estate;
(Ah, let us mourn, for never morrow
  Shall dawn upon him, desolate!) […]
VI. And travellers now within that valley,
  Through the red-litten windows see
Vast forms that move fantastically
  To a discordant melody. […]

While-reading Activities II

Worksheet Nature/Mankind/Technology – Yet Another Place

Tasks:

1. Sum up the facts about this city and its purpose.
2. Would you like to have a self-driving car? Give reasons for your answer.
3. Discuss with your neighbour if you would like to live in such a fully automatized town, and in a house like the one Ray Bradbury describes in *August 2026: There Will Come Soft Rains*. Present your conclusions.
4. Read the newsflash about applications for a Mars expedition in 2023. Discuss what makes people apply for life on Mars. Find out more about Mars One.
5. Refer your findings to Bradbury's short story *August 2026: There Will Come Soft Rains*. It is the last but one in his *Martian Chronicles*.

Extract: Scientific Ghost City to Test Future Technology

Sky News, 9 May 2012

A "world first" $1bn scientific ghost city will be built in New Mexico to test the latest next-generation technology. Researchers will use the facility in Lea County, near Hobbs, to look at everything from intelligent traffic systems and next-generation wireless networks to automated washing machines and self-flushing toilets.

The town will be modelled on the real city of Rock Hill, South Carolina, complete with roads, houses and commercial buildings, old and new. No one will live there, although they could as houses will include all the necessities, like appliances and plumbing.

The point of the town is to enable researchers to test new technologies on existing infrastructure without interfering in everyday life. For instance, while some researchers will be testing smart technologies on old grids, others might be using the streets to test self-driving cars.

Hobbs Mayor Sam Cobb said: "It brings so many great opportunities and puts us on a world stage." The city will be built by Pegasus Holdings and its New Mexico subsidiary, CITE[1] Development. The project is expected to create 350 permanent jobs and about 3,500 indirect jobs in its design, development, construction and ongoing operational phases.

* * *

Newsflash: Mars Expedition Already Draws Nearly 80,000 Applicants, May 2013

The opportunity to travel to Mars is certainly a once in a lifetime offer. More so if you're accepted to the Mars One project: the journey is a one-way ticket, requiring you to spend the rest of your life on the Red Planet. But the prospect of permanent colonization millions of miles from earth isn't thwarting[2] the hopeful, reports TIME. Almost 80,000 people have applied for the chance in just two weeks.

1 CITE = Centre for Innovation, Technology and Testing
2 to thwart: to daunt

While-reading Activities II

Worksheet Survival – *Duck and Cover*

Tasks:

1. While viewing the short film, take notes of what happens. What practice does "duck and cover" describe? Is it considered effective?
   Find the film here: http://en.wikipedia.org/wiki/Duck_and_cover
2. Discuss your list with your neighbour. In class, present your ideas about how the audience might have reacted. How would you have reacted?

Movie poster: Turtle Bert shows how to ***Duck and Cover***.

For the teacher:

Duck and Cover was a method suggested for personal protection against the effects of a nuclear weapon, which the United States government taught to generations of school children from the early 1950s into the 1980s. This was supposed to protect them in the event of an unexpected nuclear attack, which, they were told, could come at any time without any warning. Immediately after seeing a flash they had to stop what they were doing and get on the ground under some cover – such as a table, or at least next to a wall – and assume the fetal position, lying face-down and covering their heads and necks with clothes or their hands. In 1950, during the first big Civil Defense push of the Cold War, the movie ***Duck and Cover*** was produced by the Federal Civil Defense Administration for school showings in 1951. The turtle Bert shows how to "disappear" in dangerous situations. Duck-and-cover exercises quickly became a part of Civil Defense drills that every American citizen, from children to the elderly, practised to be ready in the event of nuclear war.

At that time, it was believed the main dangers of a Hiroshima-type nuclear blast were from heat and blast damage, which ***Duck and Cover*** shows plainly. Only in later publications is radiation pointed out as very dangerous. Now "Duck and Cover" is seen as a first response, assuming that after the initial blast, a person who ducks and covers will move to a more sheltered area, as – within a considerable radius and depending on the explosion's height and yield – ducking and covering would offer negligible protection against the intense heat, shock waves, and radiation.

The advice to "duck and cover", however, holds well in many situations where structural destabilization or debris may be expected, such as during an earthquake or tornado.

The exercises of civil defence are now seen as having less practical use than psychological use: to keep the danger of nuclear war high on the public mind, while also attempting to assure the American people that something could be done as a defence against nuclear attack.

In the United Kingdom similar instructions were given in 1964 by the *Civil Defence Information Bulletin No. 5*, and in the 1980s, by the *Protect and Survive* pamphlet series.

While-reading Activities II

Worksheet Survival – Survival Skills

Tasks:

1. Which points does this introduction to **Nuclear War Survival Skills** emphasise? Make a list.
2. Discuss with your neighbour about what you think of Chapter 16's minimum requirements and what strikes you.
3. Watch ***The Day After*** (USA 1983, 126 min.) and point out how the film treats the topic.
4. Prepare a talk on nuclear disarmament; mention the Intermediate-Range Nuclear Forces Treaty (INF 1987), Reagan and Gorbachev.

Extract: Self-help Civil Defense

Introduction to **Nuclear War Survival Skills**, 1987

Your best hope of surviving a nuclear war in this century is self-help civil defense – knowing the basic facts about nuclear weapon effects and what you, your family, and small groups can do to protect yourselves. Our Government continues to downgrade war-related survival preparations and spends only a few cents a year to protect each American against possible war dangers. During the 10 years or more before the Strategic Defense Initiative (Star Wars) weapons can be invented, developed and deployed, self-help civil defense will continue to be our main hope of surviving if we suffer a nuclear attack.

Most Americans hope that Star Wars will lead to the deployment of new weapons capable of destroying attacking missiles and warheads in flight. However, no defensive system can be made leak-proof. If Star Wars, presently only a research project, leads to a deployed defensive system, then self-help civil defense will be a vital part of our hoped for, truly defensive system to prevent aggression and to reduce losses if deterrence fails.

This book is written for the majority of Americans who want to improve their chances of surviving a nuclear war, it brings together field-tested instructions that have enabled untrained Americans to make expedient[3] fallout shelters, air pumps to ventilate and cool shelters, fallout meters, and other expedient life-support equipment. Also described are expedient ways to remove even dissolved radioiodine from water, and to process and cook whole grains and soybeans, our main food reserves. Successive versions of these instructions have been used successfully by families working under simulated crisis conditions, and have been improved repeatedly by Oak Ridge National Laboratory civil defense researchers and others over a period of 14 years. These improved instructions are the heart of this updated 1987 edition of the original Oak Ridge National Laboratory survival book first published in 1979.

The average American has far too little information that would help him and his family and our country survive a nuclear attack, and many of his beliefs about nuclear war are both false and dangerous. Since the A-bomb blasted Hiroshima and hurled mankind into the Nuclear Age, only during a recognized crisis threatening nuclear war have most Americans been seriously interested in improving their chances of surviving a nuclear attack. Both during and following the Cuban Missile Crisis in 1962, millions of Americans built fallout shelters or tried to obtain survival information. At that time most of the available survival information was inadequate, and dangerously faulty in some respects as it still is in 1987. Widespread

[3] "Expedient" in civil defence work describes equipment that can be made by untrained citizens in 48 hours or less, while guided solely by field-tested, written instructions and using only widely available materials and tools. *(ratsam, geeignet)*

recognition of these civil defense shortcomings has contributed to the acceptance by most Americans of one or both of two false beliefs:

One of these false beliefs is that nuclear war would be such a terrible catastrophe that it is an unthinkable impossibility. If this were true, there would be no logical reason to worry about nuclear war or to make preparations to survive a nuclear attack.

The second false belief is that, if a nuclear war were to break out, it would be the end of mankind. If this were true, a rational person would not try to improve his chances of surviving the unsurvivable.

This book gives facts that show these beliefs are false. History shows that once a weapon is invented it remains ready for use in the arsenals of some nations and in time will be used. Researchers who have spent much time and effort learning the facts about effects of nuclear weapons now know that all-out nuclear war would not be the end of mankind or of civilization. Even if our country remained unprepared and were subjected to an all-out nuclear attack, many millions of Americans would survive and could live through the difficult post-attack years. [...]

The emphasis in this book is on survival preparations that can be made in the last few days of a worsening crisis. However, the measures put into effect during such a crisis can be very much more effective if plans and some preparations are completed well in advance. It is hoped that persons who read this book will be motivated at least to make the preparations outlined in Chapter 16, Minimum Pre-Crisis Preparations.

Well-informed persons realize that a nuclear attack by the Soviet Union is unlikely to be a Pearl-Harbor-type of attack, launched without warning. Strategists agree that a nuclear war most likely would begin after a period of days-to-months of worsening crisis. The most realistic of the extensive Russian plans and preparations to survive a nuclear war are based on using at least several days during an escalating crisis to get most urban dwellers out of the cities and other high risk areas, to build or improve shelters in all parts of the Soviet Union, and to protect essential machinery and the like. The Russians know that if they are able to complete evacuation and sheltering plans before the outbreak of nuclear war, the number of their people killed would be a small fraction of those who otherwise would die. Our satellites and other sources of intelligence would reveal such massive movements within a day; therefore, under the most likely circumstances, Americans would have several days in which to make life-saving preparations.

Extract: Chapter 16, Minimum Pre-Crisis Preparations

Your chances of surviving a nuclear attack will be improved if you make the following low-cost preparations before a serious crisis arises. Once many Americans become convinced that a nuclear attack is a near certainty, they will rush to stores and buy all available survival supplies. If you wait to prepare until a crisis does arise, you are likely to be among the majority who will have to make-do with inadequate supplies of water containers, food, and materials. Furthermore, even if you have the necessary materials and instructions to make the most needed survival items, you and your family are not likely to have time to make all of them during a few days of tense crisis.

The following recommendations are intended primarily for the majority who live in areas likely to be subjected to blast, fire, or extremely heavy fallout. These people should plan to evacuate to a safer area. (Many citizens living outside high-risk areas, especially homeowners with yards, can and should make better pre-crisis preparations. These would include building high-protection-factor permanent shelters covered with earth.)

Shelter
Keep on hand the tools and materials your family or group will need to build or improve a high-protection-factor expedient shelter: One or more shovels, a pick (if in a hard-soil area), a bow-saw with an extra blade, a hammer, and 4-mil polyethylene film for rainproofing your planned shelter. Also store the necessary nails, wire, etc., needed for the kind of shelter you plan to build.

Keep instructions for shelter-building and other survival essentials in a safe and convenient place.

Ventilation-cooling
Make a homemade shelter-ventilating pump, a KAP[4], of the size required for the shelter you plan to build or use.

Water
Keep on hand water containers (including at least four 30-gallon untreated polyethylene trash bags and two sacks or pillowcases for each person), a pliable garden hose or other tube for siphoning, and a plastic bottle of sodium hypochlorite bleach (such as Clorox) for disinfecting water and utensils.

Fallout meter
Make one or two KFMs[5] and learn how to use this simple instrument.

Food
Store at least a 2-week supply of compact, nonperishable food. The balanced ration of basic dry foods described in Chapter 9, Food, satisfies requirements for adults and larger children at minimum cost. If your family includes babies or small children, be sure to store more milk powder, vegetable oil, and sugar. Continuing to breast-feed babies born during an impending crisis would greatly simplify their care should the crisis develop and worsen.

For preparing and cooking basic foods:
- Make a 3-Pipe Grain Mill like the one described in Chapter 9, Food, or buy a small hand-cranked grain mill, which grinds more efficiently than other expedient devices.
- Make a Bucket-Stove as described in Chapter 9. During evacuation, the stove can be used as a container. Store some kitchen-type wooden matches in a waterproof container.
- Keep essential containers and utensils on hand for storing and transporting food and for cooking and serving in a shelter.

Sanitation
A hose-vented 5-gallon can, with heavy plastic bags for liners, for use as a toilet. Include some smaller plastic bags and toilet paper with these supplies. Tampons.
Insect screen or mosquito netting, and fly bait. See Chapter 12.

Medicines
- Any special medications needed by family members.
- Potassium iodide, a 2-oz bottle, and a medicine-dropper, for prophylactic protection of the thyroid gland against radioactive iodines. (Described in the last section of Chapter 14, Survival Without Doctors)
- A first-aid kit and a tube of antibiotic ointment.

Light
- Long-burning candles (with small wicks) sufficient for at least 14 nights.
- An expedient lamp, with extra cotton-string, wicks, and cooking oil as described in Chapter 11.
- A flashlight and extra batteries.

Radio
A transistor radio with extra batteries and a metal box in which to protect it.

Other Essentials
Review the EVACUATION CHECKLIST (developed primarily for persons who make no preparations before a crisis) and add items that are special requirements of your family.

Find more at: www.oism.org/nwss/s73p927.htm

[4] KAP – Kearny Air Pump
[5] KFM – Kearny Fallout Meter

While-reading Activities II

Worksheet Survival – *Doomsday Preppers*

Tasks:

1. What is the series *Doomsday Preppers* about? Refer to their website and the extract below.
2. Group the test questions according to categories. Point out how much emphasis is placed on each item and what might be missing.
   Can you find a similar test for German citizens?
3. Discuss with your neighbour what you think of doomsday and Zombie apocalypse preparations (p. 41). Present your views to the class.

About the show *Doomsday Preppers*

Doomsday Preppers explores the lives of otherwise ordinary Americans who are preparing for the end of the world as we know it. Unique in their beliefs, motivations, and strategies, preppers will go to whatever lengths they can to make sure they are prepared for any of life's uncertainties. And with our expert's assessment, they will find out their chances of survival if their worst fears become a reality.

Test: How prepped are you? (Go to the website provided below to do the test.)

How long would you survive after a global cataclysm? We've seen what it takes to prepare for the worst, and for some it's a full-time job. You've watched the preppers get their scores, now it's your turn.

We are evaluating you on the same scale as the Doomsday Preppers to rule how long you will survive, and where you stand on the prepper leaderboard. From water supply to shelter location and security, all aspects of prepping are interconnected. Keep a close eye on your score as you progress to see how your answers affect your rating from question to question and apply to your overall score. Along the way, we'll provide survival tips for you to improve your score. Already feel like a prepping-pro? See how you stack against the Doomsday Preppers.

1. How many gallons of water do you have stored per person? (1 gallon = 3.8 litres)	
2. Do you have a renewable water supply?	
3. How far away is your renewable water supply?	
4. Do you have a means to purify your water supply?	
5. How much food do you have stored per person?	meats/fruit & vegetables/grains/ MRE (Meals Ready to Eat)
6. Do you have a renewable food supply?	garden/orchard/livestock/fish
7. Do you have a means to replenish food supply?	canning/jarring/dehydrating/ year-round-gardening
8. What kind of climate do you live in?	
9. How densely populated is your location? (Population density affects the safety of resources.)	
10. Do you have a bunker or safe room? (Should be stocked and prepared for disaster/invaders)	

11. Do you have a means to generate electricity?	
12. Do you have a means to heat/cool your location?	wood/propane/solar/geo-thermal
13. Do you have a means to cook food at your location? (Should be off-grid and renewable)	
14. Do you have a bug-out location (=a refuge)? (This refuge should be self-sufficient, easily defended, and generally located in a lightly populated rural area.)	
15. Do you have enough fuel to get there?	
16. Do you have a plan for the bug-out location? (account for supplies and security)	
17. Do you have any specialized training?	
18. What is your level of expertise?	Basic/Intermediate/SWAT-Special Forces
19. How many firearms do you own?	
20. Do you have standardized weapons? (They use the same ammunition.)	
21. How much ammo have you stored for each weapon?	
22. Do you have any security enhancements?	night vision/body armour/nuclear biological and chemical protection gear/fortification/ surveillance/ non-lethal weapons
23. How many able-bodied preppers are in your group?	
24. What is the average survival skill level for your group?	untrained/weekend camper/survivalist
25. Are you prepared for a medical emergency?	stored antibiotics/medicine/ medical supplies/kit
26. Are you medically trained?	Basic First Aid/Intermediate/EM
27. Do you have a means of communication?	short-range radio/walkie talkies/ long-range radio/short-wave radio
28. Do you have a bug-out vehicle? In the event of a major crisis, you may need to leave your primary refuge.	
29. Do you have enough fuel and capacity for your group and supplies?	
30. Does the vehicle have 4-wheel drive?	
31. Do you have items for bartering?	extra ammo/extra food/extra medical supplies/alcohol and/or tobacco/currency (Silver is the most readily tradable.)
32. How well can you handle an emergency? (High stress situations require a sound mind and body.)	

Get the free App

Design a multi-level dream bunker complete with all you need for post-apocalyptic bliss

http://channel.nationalgeographic.com/channel/doomsday-preppers/interactives/how-prepped-are-you1/

Oct. 22, 2012

Extra task: Discuss the contents of this survival set with your neighbour. Who might buy this?

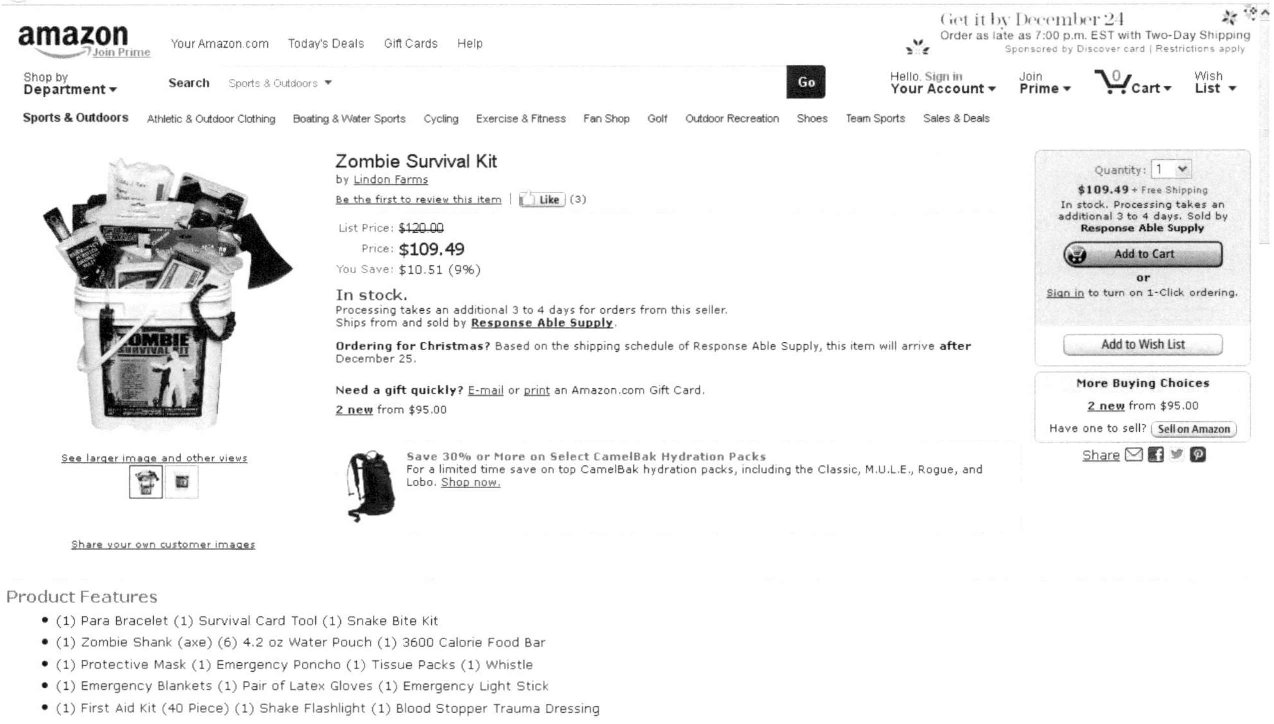

The survival bucket contains (as listed in Product Features):

1 Para Bracelet, 1 Survival Card Tool, 1 Snake Bite Kit, 1 Zombie Shank (axe), 6 4.2 oz Water pouches, 1 3600 Calorie Food Bar, 1 Protective Mask, 1 Emergency Poncho, 1 Tissue Packs, 1 Whistle, 1 Emergency Blanket, 1 Pair of Latex Gloves, 1 Emergency Light Stick, 1 First Aid Kit (40 Piece), 1 Shake Flashlight, 1 Blood Stopper Trauma Dressing

For the teacher:

The questions about doomsday preparations can be divided into water, food, shelter, security, transport, and additional factors like health care, trading and communication.

There seems to be a high emphasis on weapons and on defending the group's shelter.
What seems to be missing are preparations for additional toilet facilities. The scenario assumes that there isn't any electricity or running water. This means that waste disposal should be considered, too.

A good survivalist has the same qualities as a pioneer and settler in the 19th century: self-reliant, resilient, and well-armed.

Worksheet Survival – Zombie Apocalypse

Tasks:

1. Why do the title and the text mention zombies?
2. Discuss if this message would work in Germany. Suggest alternatives.
3. What attitude does the author of the article express? Give proof.

Extract: Seriously? Government warns citizens of 'zombie apocalypse' to urge better emergency plans

Alicia A. Caldwell, The Associated Press, 7 September 2012

Washington – "The zombies are coming!" the Homeland Security Department says.

Tongue firmly in cheek, the government urged citizens Thursday to prepare for a zombie apocalypse, part of a public health campaign to encourage better preparation for genuine disasters and emergencies. The theory: If you're prepared for a zombie attack, the same preparations will help during a hurricane, pandemic, earthquake or terrorist attack.

The Federal Emergency Management Agency hosted an online seminar for its Citizen Corps organization to help emergency planners better prepare their communities for disaster. The federal Centers for Disease Control and Prevention last year first launched a zombie apocalypse social media campaigning for the same purposes.

Emergency planners were encouraged to use the threat of zombies – the flesh-hungry, walking dead – to encourage citizens to prepare for disasters.

Among the government's recommendations were having an emergency evacuation plan and a change of clothes, plus keeping on hand fresh water, extra medications and emergency flashlights.

A few of the government's suggestions tracked closely with some of the 33 rules for dealing with zombies popularized in the 2009 movie "Zombieland", which included "always carry a change of underwear" and "when in doubt, know your way out."

To the teacher:

Find more information at the sites of Centres for Disease Control and Prevention.
http://blogs.cdc.gov/publichealthmatters/2011/05/preparedness-101-zombie-apocalypse
http://www.fema.gov/plan-prepare-mitigate
http://www.oism.org/nwss/s73p927.htm
http://www.surviveprepare.com
http://www.motherearthnews.com

Check sites which poke fun at this. Search for: "How to survive a Zombie attack" and "Zombie Apocalypse".

Worksheet Survival – Emergency Plans

Tasks:

1. Summarise the recommendations in English. Go to www.bbk.bund.de to see the full texts.
2. What is not mentioned in this guideline for personal preparations for an emergency?
3. Discuss in groups how you judge this approach and if your family has made preparations for an emergency.

Extract: **Vorsorge für den Notfall**
Bundesamt für Bevölkerungsschutz und Katastrophenschutz

In den Medien wird täglich von Unfällen und Katastrophen berichtet.

Meist betrifft es andere. Aber ganz schnell können auch Sie einem Brand, Hochwasser, Chemieunfall, Stromausfall oder anderen Gefahren ausgesetzt sein.

Wenn der Notfall eingetreten ist, ist es zu spät, umfangreiche Vorsorgemaßnahmen erst zu planen. Bis Hilfe eintrifft, vergeht Zeit. Und dabei kommt es gerade dann vielleicht auf Minuten an, die über das Leben von Menschen oder den Erhalt von Sachwerten entscheiden. Minuten, in denen jeder von uns erst einmal auf sich selbst gestellt ist, in denen die Vorsorgemaßnahmen sich bewähren sollen.

Das richtige Verhalten in Notsituationen und die Vorbereitungen darauf bezeichnet man als Selbstschutz. Der Selbstschutz kann helfen, die Zeit bis zum Eintreffen der Feuerwehr, Rettungsdienst oder Katastrophenschutz zu überbrücken.

Auch können persönliche Vorsorgemaßnahmen helfen, die Auswirkungen eines Schadens auf uns und unser Umfeld zu reduzieren.

Jeder muss sich fragen: Bin ich vorbereitet?
Kann ich mir und anderen in Notsituationen helfen?

Unten stehend finden Sie Tipps, wie Sie sich auf Notsituationen vorbereiten können.

Die Broschüre „Für den Notfall vorgesorgt" (Okt. 2012) bietet Ihnen eine übersichtliche Zusammenfassung aller Vorsorgemaßnahmen.

Zu den wichtigsten Dingen, für die Sie persönlich Vorbereitungen treffen können, gehören:

Brandschutz
Durch Maßnahmen des vorbeugenden Brandschutzes können die Gefahren für Menschen und Sachwerte entscheidend verringert werden.

Dokumentensicherung
Sichern Sie Ihre Dokumente! Sind wichtige Papiere erst verloren gegangen, so ist ihre Wiederbeschaffung unter Umständen schwierig oder sogar unmöglich.

Energieausfall
Wenn Öl und Strom zusammen ausfallen, gibt es für den modernen Haushalt normalerweise keine Heiz- und Kochmöglichkeiten mehr. Bei einem Energieausfall helfen Campingkocher und stromunabhängige Heizgeräte.

Hausapotheke
Alles, was ein Kfz-Verbandkasten enthält, von der Mull-Kompresse über Verbandschere, Wunddesinfektionsmittel, Pflaster, Binden bis zum Dreiecktuch empfiehlt sich auch für Ihre Hausapotheke.

Hygiene
Auch unter erschwerten Bedingungen sollte die Körperpflege konsequent weiter durchgeführt werden. In jeden Haushalt gehört daher ein ausreichender Vorrat an Seife, Waschmittel und Zahnpasta.

Lebensmittel
Jeder Haushalt sollte sich für alle Fälle einen Vorrat anlegen, der für ein bis zwei Wochen ausreicht und aus Lebensmittel und Getränken besteht, die auch ohne Kühlung länger lagerfähig sind.

Notgepäck
Mit Notgepäck das Haus verlassen – Zweckmäßigstes Transportmittel ist ein Rucksack, der auch ohne fremde Hilfe längere Zeit getragen werden kann.

Informationsquelle Radio
Viele Rundfunkgeräte können sowohl über Netzanschluss als auch mit Batterien betrieben werden. Damit können Sie auch bei Stromausfall noch informiert werden.

Checkliste Notgepäck:

Notgepäck

Was ist bereits vorhanden?

	vorhanden	**beschaffen**
persönliche Medikamente		
Behelfsmäßige Schutzkleidung		
Wolldecke / Schlafsack		
Unterwäsche u. Strümpfe		
Gummistiefel, derbes Schuhwerk		
Essgeschirr/-besteck, Thermoskanne, Becher		
Material zur Wundversorgung		
Dosenöffner und Taschenmesser		
strapazierfähige, warme Kleidung		
Taschenlampe		
Kopfbedeckung, Schutzhelm		
Schutzmaske, behelfsmäßiger Atemschutz		
Arbeitshandschuhe		

(Quelle: Booklet „Für den Notfall vorgesorgt“, p. 44)

While-reading Activities II

Worksheet Survival – Secret Tests

Tasks:

1. Why are these tests which were carried out in the 1950s relevant now?
2. What does Lisa Martino-Taylor want to achieve?
3. Explain and discuss the mindset behind these tests, the Duck and Cover campaign, etc.

Extract: Secret Cold War tests in St. Louis raise concerns
Jim Salter, Associated Press, 4 October 2012

ST. LOUIS – Doris Spates was a baby when her father died inexplicably in 1955. She has watched four siblings die of cancer, and she survived cervical cancer.

After learning that the Army conducted secret chemical testing in her impoverished St. Louis neighborhood at the height of the Cold War, she wonders if her own government is to blame.

In the mid-1950s, and again a decade later, the Army used motorized blowers atop a low-income housing high-rise, at schools and from the backs of station wagons to send a potentially dangerous compound into the already-hazy air in predominantly black areas of St. Louis.

Local officials were told at the time that the government was testing a smoke screen that could shield St. Louis from aerial observation in case the Russians attacked.

But in 1994, the government said the tests were part of a biological weapons program and St. Louis was chosen because it bore some resemblance to Russian cities the U.S. might atttack. The material being sprayed was zinc cadmium sulfide, a fine fluorescent powder.

Now, new research is raising greater concern about the implications of those tests. St. Louis Community College-Meramec sociology professor Lisa Martino-Taylor's research has raised the possibility that the Army performed radiation testing by mixing radioactive particles with the zinc cadmium sulfide, though she concedes there is no direct proof.

The area of the secret testing is described by the Army in documents obtained by Martino-Taylor through a Freedom of Information Act request as "a densely populated slum district." About three-quarters of the residents were black.

Martino-Taylor decided to research the testing for her doctoral thesis at the University of Missouri. She believes the St. Louis study was linked to the Manhattan Atomic Bomb Project and a small group of scientists from that project who were developing radiological weapons. A congressional study in 1993 confirmed radiological testing in Tennessee and part of the West during the Cold War.

Martino-Taylor said a follow-up health study should be performed in St. Louis, but it must involve direct input from people who lived in the targeted areas. "Their voices have not been heard."

While-reading Activities II

Worksheet Survival – *The Machine Stops*

Tasks:

1. What do these extracts express?
2. How do you think Kuno's story will go on?
3. a) Draw what happened to Kuno.
   b) Compare your drawings with the students' drawings provided.
4. Read the story in the students' book, pp. 24–39. Did you expect this ending?

Extracts: The Machine Stops

E. M. Forster, 1909

I. *Kuno is telling his mother Vashti what he thinks of the Machine that is controlling their underground world.*

His voice rose passionately. "Cannot you see, cannot all you lecturers see, that it is we that are dying, and that down here the only thing that really lives is the Machine? We created the Machine, to do our will, but we cannot make it do our will now. It has robbed us of the sense of space and of the sense of touch, it has blurred every human relation and narrowed down love to a carnal act, it has paralysed our bodies and our wills, and now it compels us to worship it.

"The Machine develops – but not on our lines. The Machine proceeds – but not to our goal. We only exist as the blood corpuscles that course through its arteries, and if it could work without us, it would let us die."

Kuno above ground

II. *Kuno's secret excursion above ground to the hills of Wessex takes an abrupt ending, when the Machine's Mending Apparatus captures him and drags him back through the shaft.*

"I thought I heard a faint scraping noise in the depths. At this – but it was too late – I took alarm. I realized that something evil was at work, and I had better escape to the outer air, and, if I must die, die running towards the cloud that had been the colour of a pearl. I never started. Out of the shaft – it is too horrible. A worm, a long white worm, had crawled out of the shaft and was gliding over the moonlit grass.

"I screamed. I did everything that I should not have done. I stamped upon the creature instead of flying from it, and it at once curled round the ankle. Then we fought. The worm let me run all over the dell, but edged up my leg as I ran. "Help!" I cried. "Help!" When my feet were wound together, I fell, I was dragged away from the dear ferns and the living hills, and past the great metal stopper. The last things that I saw, ere the stopper closed after us, were certain stars, and I felt that a man of my sort lived in the sky. For I did fight, I fought till the very end, and it was only my head hitting against the ladder that quieted me. I woke up in this room. The worms had vanished. I was surrounded by artificial air, artificial light, artificial peace."

"The Machine has been most merciful", she said.
"I prefer the mercy of God."

The repair worms

While-reading Activities III

Worksheet Response to Tragedy – Writing poems

Task:

Write an eleven-word poem about DEATH. You can work in little groups, too.
Use this format: one word in line 1, two words in line 2, three words in line 3, four words in line 4 and one word, summarising your ideas, in the fifth and last line. Present and explain your poem.

These are some poems written by students. Compare them with yours.

Everybody
Has to
Deal with it.
Death is part of
Life.

Death
Carpe Diem
Seize the Day
A Part of Life
End.

Death.
Is this
the end of
Life or is there
more?

Death.
Feeling sad.
Losing your hopes.
Accepting. Making the best
of Life.

You
gonna die.
Scared of dying.
But freedom by accepting
Death.

Death
You die
I'm dying too.
We will all die.
Mortals.

Death
Life starts
And it ends.
There's no way out.
Peace

Someday
It comes
Takes you away
To a different world.
Death.

And another format:

Gestern lebt' ich,
Heute leid' ich,
Morgen sterb' ich;
Dennoch denk' ich
Heut' und morgen
Gern an gestern
Gotthold Ephraim Lessing
(1729–1781)

death
death
death death **hope** death death
death
death
death
death

While-reading Activities III

Worksheet Response to Tragedy – The Sick Rose

Tasks:

1. Which topics can you find in the poem below? Exchange your thoughts with your neighbour. Explain what is most important for you.
2. Find reasons why Blake includes this poem in the cycle “Songs of Experience”.

The Sick Rose (1794)
by William Blake (1757–1827)
from **Songs of Experience**

O Rose, thou art sick!
The invisible worm
That flies in the night,
In the howling storm,

Has found out thy bed
Of crimson joy;
And his dark secret love
Does thy life destroy.

For the teacher:

The following topics can be found in William Blake’s poem:
illness, love, nature, relationship, desire, sex, loss, destruction, death

Students lay their emphases differently. This poem will make students defend their ways of seeing and understanding it. Their individual answers show what preoccupies them most and what is most evident to them.

While-reading Activities III

Worksheet Response to Tragedy – The Icarus myth

Tasks:

1. With your partner, imagine situations in which a child dies. List possible reactions of the parents and of others and present them to the class.
2. Sum up what you have found out about Icarus from the short entry below. Use additional information from your students' book, pp. 40–42.
3. Make a drawing of Icarus' fall.
4. Compare the Bruegel painting (students' book, p. 43) with your drawing. Discuss with your partner what the painter emphasised and if it differs from your view.

The Icarus myth

Icarus' father Daedalus, a talented and remarkable Athenian craftsman, built the Labyrinth for King Minos of Crete, near his palace at Knossos, to imprison the Minotaur, a half-man, half-bull monster born of his wife and the Cretan bull.

Minos imprisoned Daedalus himself in the labyrinth because he had given Minos' daughter Ariadne a ball of string in order to help Theseus, the enemy of Minos, to survive the Labyrinth and defeat the Minotaur.

In order to escape Daedalus fashioned two pairs of wings out of wax and feathers for himself and his son. Daedalus tried his wings first, but before taking off from the island, warned his son not to fly too close to the sun, nor too close to the sea, but to follow his path of flight. Overcome by the giddiness that flying lent him, Icarus soared through the sky curiously, but in the process he came too close to the sun, which melted the wax. Icarus kept flapping his wings but soon realized that he had no feathers left and that he was only flapping his bare arms, and so Icarus fell into the sea in the area which today bears his name, the Icarian Sea near Icaria, an island southwest of Samos.

While-reading Activities III

Worksheet Response to Tragedy – *Musée des Beaux Arts*

Tasks:

1. Find information on the Icarus myth and retell it in your own words.
2. Describe the Brueghel painting (students' book, p. 43).
3. Underline key words in the poem (students' book, pp. 54–55).
4. In which context are suffering and martyrdom mentioned?
5. Who are the people mentioned in the poem and what are they doing?
6. What feelings does this poem evoke in you? Sum up its message in one line or a phrase.
7. How does William Carlos Williams deal with the Icarus myth in his poem? Refer to students' book, pp. 57–59. Explain which of the poems you prefer and why.

Poem: **Musée des Beaux Arts**
W.H. Auden

Auden wrote this poem after having seen the paintings "Landscape with the Fall of Icarus" and "The Census in Bethlehem" by Pieter Brueghel (16th century) in the Museum of Fine Arts in Brussels in 1938.

About suffering they were never wrong,
The Old Masters; how well they understood
Its human position; how it takes place
While someone else is eating or opening a window or just walking dully along;
How, when the aged are reverently, passionately waiting
For the miraculous birth, there always must be
Children who did not specially want it to happen, skating
On a pond at the edge of the wood:
They never forgot
That even the most dreadful martyrdom must run its course
Anyhow in a corner, some untidy spot
Where the dogs go on with their doggy life and the torturer's horse
Scratches its innocent behind on a tree.
In Brueghel's Icarus, for instance: how everything turns away
Quite leisurely from the disaster; the ploughman may
Have heard the splash, the forsaken cry,
But for him it was not an important failure; the sun shone
As it had to on the white legs disappearing into the green
Water; and the expensive delicate ship that must have seen
Something amazing, a boy falling out of the sky,
Had somewhere to get to and sailed calmly on.

For the teacher:

ad 4:
Suffering is seen as a part of life, and depicted as such by the Old Masters. It is not especially heroic, or even remarkable – it exists while others are busy with their own lives and do not care. They go about their own business and do not even look.

ad 5:
In the first lines of the poem Auden states that the Old Master gave a correct judgment of the indifference of people when others suffer. They continue to eat, look out of the window, walk along while miracles and tragedies happen.

In the first part of the poem he refers to Brueghel's painting *The Census at Bethlehem* (students' book, p. 44). Old people, believers, are waiting for Christ's birth, whereas young people and children – who have their lives before them – are not interested and are skating on a pond. The birth of the Messiah, one of the central events in Christendom, is not relevant for them.
Nor is Christ's martyrdom and death. In an "untidy spot", a banal place, with the executioner's horse and an itching dog for company, the Saviour's life ends. It is not spectacular at all.

The second part refers to Brueghel's painting *Landscape with the Fall of Icarus* (students' book, p. 43). The ploughman continues to plough the field. He does not even turn to see the cause of the splash in the water, nor do the sailors bother to inquire and to stop their ship.

ad 6:
Individual answers.
"Nobody cares."

ad 7:
Williams' poem is more straightforward. It is geared towards facts. One can easily recreate Brueghel's painting with his descriptive lines.

This very unemotional way of imparting the facts mirrors the poem's message. There is no warmth, no caring and no feeling. This comes across as a more modern conception of showing suffering.

While-reading Activities III

Worksheet Response to Tragedy – Death and the Artist

Tasks:

1. Find information on Andy Warhol and present the artist.
2. Describe and explain his *Self-Portrait with Skull*. Include the concept of *Memento Mori*.

Andy Warhol,
Self-Portrait with Skull
(1978)

3. Work in groups. Present and explain the following paintings.
   Point out when Andy Warhol created them as a reaction to which events.

   Group 1: Skulls (1976)
   Group 2: Paratrooper Boots (1985–86)
   Group 3: Map of Eastern U.S.S.R. Missile Bases (1985–86)
   Group 4: Airborne. We Kill for Peace (1985–86)
   Group 5: Camouflage (1986)

For the teacher:

Andy Warhol, in the last ten years of his life, created several cycles in which he focussed on the topics of death and religion, from the *Skull* series of 1976 to *The Last Supper* paintings of 1986.

The ***Skull*** paintings of 1976 are not specifically religious, although the related ***Self-portrait with Skull*** paintings of 1978 suggest that Warhol was working within the *memento mori* tradition. The skull paintings are based on a photograph of an actual skull that Warhol bought in Paris. It is important to note that in the skull series, Warhol uses bright cheerful colours – red, blue, yellow, green – and not the traditionally used browns of *memento mori* paintings. Death is not a subject to be avoided and feared but a part of life.

The following three paintings were all created in 1985–86.

The mid-1980s was a period in which Cold War tension between the Soviet Union and the United States increased and in which President Ronald Reagan referred to the Soviet Union as the "Evil Empire" (in a speech to the National Association of Evangelicals on March 8, 1983) and called for a "Strategic Defence Initiative" (popularly known as 'Star Wars') to "defend America from Soviet missiles". In his painting ***Map of Eastern U.S.S.R. Missile Bases*** Andy Warhol specifically refers to this.

The diptych ***Paratrooper Boots*** shows that the US is ready to meet the challenge.
The same is expressed in the painting ***Airborne. We Kill for Peace***.
All these series and paintings show the renewed fear of nuclear war and American readiness to strike (back).

The ***Camouflage*** series, which Warhol called his 'war pictures', obviously take their inspiration from military camouflage patterns. But as he paints them in red, pink, orange, yellow and blue he undermines the military aspect of camouflage, which, by imitating natural colours – khaki, green, ochre – allows the soldiers to melt into their surroundings.

Is this camouflage effective? Which animals use camouflage? Can camouflage be seen as a metaphor for hiding one's real self away?

Students can discuss if they see happy images in bright colours, jigsaw pieces of a world which will never fit together, a heap of bodies or a big group of happy dancers. They can figure out if they see humans or animals, if they see the camouflage series as threatening, ironic, …

While-reading Activities IV

Worksheet Letting Go or Holding Tight – Quotes

Tasks:

1. Choose one of the quotations. Write an essay explaining why this fits your attitude.
2. Make photographs or a drawing to show your view of life. Present them to the others.

Some quotes:

1. *When one door closes another door opens; but we so often look so long and so regretfully upon the closed door that we do not see the ones which open for us.* Alexander Graham Bell

2. *Some of us think holding on makes us strong, but sometimes it is letting go.* Herman Hesse

3. *One problem with gazing too frequently into the past is that we may turn around to find the future has run out on us.* Michael Cibenko

4. *All the art of living is a fine mingling of letting go and holding on.* Havelock Ellis

5. *Death leaves a heartache no one can heal, love leaves a memory no one can steal.* (headstone)

6. *Change is never easy, you fight to hold on, and you fight to let go.* The Wonder Years

7. *Every exit is an entry somewhere.* Tom Stoppard

8. *There's no need to miss someone from your past. There's a reason they didn't make it to your future.* (unknown)

9. *There are things that we never want to let go of, people we never want to leave behind. But keep in mind that letting go isn't the end of the world, it's the beginning of a new life.*

10. *When I let go of what I am, I become what I might be.* Lao Tzu

11. *We must be willing to let go of the life we have planned, so as to accept the life that is waiting for us.* Joseph Campbell

12. *Let go, in order to achieve. Letting go is God's law.* Mary Manin Morrissey

13. *Hold on tight to your dream*
    Hold on tight to your dream
    When you see the shadows falling
    When you hear that cold wind calling
    Hold on tight to your dream Electric Light Orchestra, 1981

14. *Ashes to ashes, funk to funky*
    We know Major Tom's a junkie David Bowie, 1980

15. *Death ends a life, not a relationship.* Jack Lemmon

16. *We cannot prevent the birds of sorrow from flying over our heads but we can refuse to let them build nests in our hair.* Ron Schreiber, "The Birds of Sorrow"

17. *To hold, you must first open your hand. Let go.* Lao Tzu

18. *Love knows not its own depth until the hour of separation.* Khalil Gibran

19. *Grief is like the ocean; it comes on waves ebbing and flowing. Sometimes the water is calm, and sometimes it is overwhelming. All we can do is learn to swim.* Vicki Harrison

20. *Death is not the end, it is simply walking out of the physical form and into the spirit realm, which is our true home. It's going back home.* Stephen Christopher

21. *There is a sacredness in tears. They are not the mark of weakness, but of power. They speak more eloquently than ten thousand tongues. They are messengers of overwhelming grief and unspeakable love.* Washington Irving

22. *Just as a little bird cracks open the shell and flies out, we fly out of this shell, the shell of the body. We call that death, but strictly speaking, death is nothing but a change of form.* Swami Satchidananda

23. *Don't be dismayed at goodbyes, a farewell is necessary before you can meet again; and meeting again, after moments or lifetimes, is certain for those who are friends.* Richard Bach

While-reading Activities IV

Worksheet Letting Go or Holding Tight – Time Eternal

Tasks:

1. Look at the memorial tributes and discuss with your neighbour if you would place similar tributes in a newspaper. What attitudes do they show?

In Memory of May 2002
....

It will never be as it was …
Missing you,
With love ....

Without you ....
A year has gone by (1955–2012)
We are slowly awoken by reality
Emerging from the dark
Realizing the world hasn't changed
And yet everything is different
Without you.

2. John Dowland's song shows his approach to life and death. Sum it up in a few lines and connect it with the ideas of *Memento Mori* and *Carpe Diem*. Show links to Auden's poem *Musée des Beaux Arts*.

Poem: **O what hath overwrought,** from Third Book of Songs
John Dowland (1563–1626)

O what hath overwrought (1603)	**Modern transformation**
O what hath overwrought	Oh, what has wearied and exhausted
My all amazed thought	my bewildered mind?
Or whereto am I brought,	To what end have I been brought,
That thus in vaine have sought,	I who have searched in vain,
Till time and truth hath taught,	Until Time and Truth have taught me that
I labor all for nought.	my previous efforts have all been for nothing.
The day I see is cleare,	The day that I now see is clear,
But I am nere the neere	but I am never any nearer (to my happiness),
For griefe doth still appeare,	for Grief is still present,
To crosse our merie cheere,	to counter any merry expressions.
While I ken nothing heare,	At present I experience nothing here
But winter all the yeare.	but winter all the year round.
Cold, hold,	O Coldness, stop!
The sun will shine warme,	The sun will shine warmly again –
Therfore now feare no harme.	Therefore fear no harm.
O blessed beames,	O blessed rays (of the Spring sun)
Where beautie streames	where Beauty shines,
Happie light to loves dreames.	the happy light/torch to dreams of love.

While-reading Activities IV

Worksheet Letting Go or Holding Tight – The Afterlife

Tasks:

1. What does Dr. Eben Alexander say about the afterlife? Refer to Extracts 1 and 3.
2. How do Eric Pfeiffer and MSN Now present this in Extracts 1 and 2?
3. How do the various religions present the afterlife?
4. Tell your thoughts about the afterlife to your neighbour and share them with the class.

Extract 1: Heaven is real, says neurosurgeon

Eric Pfeiffer, Yahoo! News, 9 October 2012

Dr. Eben Alexander has taught at Harvard Medical School and has earned a strong reputation as a neurosurgeon. And while Alexander says he's long called himself a Christian, he never held deeply religious beliefs or a pronounced faith in the afterlife.

But after a week in a coma during the fall of 2008, during which his neocortex ceased to function, Alexander claims he experienced a life-changing visit to the afterlife, specifically heaven.

"According to current medical understanding of the brain and mind, there is absolutely no way that I could have experienced even a dim and limited consciousness during my time in the coma, much less the hyper-vivid and completely coherent odyssey I underwent," Alexander writes in the cover story of this week's edition of Newsweek.

So what exactly does heaven look like?

Alexander says he first found himself floating above clouds before witnessing, "transparent, shimmering beings arced across the sky, leaving strong, streamer-like lines behind them."
He claims to have been escorted by an unknown female companion and says communicated with these beings through a method of correspondence that transcended language. Alexander says the messages he received from those beings loosely translated as:

"You are loved and cherished, dearly, forever."
"You have nothing to fear."
"There is nothing you can do wrong."

From there, Alexander claims to have traveled to "an immense void, completely dark, infinite in size, yet also infinitely comforting." He believes this void was the home of God.

After recovering from his meningitis-induced coma, Alexander says he was reluctant to share his experience with his colleagues but found comfort inside the walls of this church. He's chronicled his experience in a new book, "Proof of Heaven: A neurosurgeon's journey into the afterlife", which will be published in late October.

"I'm still a doctor, and still a man of science every bit as much as I was before I had my experience," Alexander writes. "But on a deep level I'm very different from the person I was before, because I have caught a glimpse of this emerging picture of reality. And you can believe me when I tell you that it will be worth every bit of the work it will take us, and those who come after us, to get it right."

Extract 2: Neurosurgeon says he has proof heaven is real, describes it

MSN Now – What's Trending, 10 October 2012

Most of us probably assumed we wouldn't get a definitive answer to the question of whether heaven is real until we were no longer able to ask, but in an ultra-trippy Newsweek cover story, neuroscientist Dr. Eben Alexander claims to have incontrovertible proof that heaven actually exists. How does he know? He had a bacterial infection that shut down his neocortex, and while in a coma, he saw "a place of clouds. Big, puffy, pink-white ones" and he traveled on a butterfly wing with a young woman with "high cheekbones," "deep-blue eyes" and "golden brown tresses" who told him he was loved, safe and could do no wrong. Whoa, that was some coma.

Extract 3: Questions Are Answered

Dr. Eben Alexander, Newsweek, 8 October 2012

A warm wind blew through, like the kind that springs up on the most perfect summer days, tossing the leaves of the trees and flowing past like heavenly water. A divine breeze. It changed everything, shifting the world around me into an even higher octave, a higher vibration.

I began wordlessly putting questions to this wind and to the divine being that I sensed at work behind it or within it.

Where is this place?

Who am I?

Why am I here?

Each time I silently put one of these questions out, the answer came instantly in an explosion of light, color, love and beauty that blew through me like a crashing wave. What was important about these blasts was that they didn't simply silence my questions by overwhelming them. They answered them, but in a way that bypassed language. Thoughts entered me directly. But it wasn't thought like we experience on earth. It wasn't vague, immaterial, or abstract. These thoughts were solid and immediate – hotter than fire and wetter than water – and as I received them I was able to instantly and effortlessly understand concepts that would have taken me years to fully grasp in my earthly life.

I continued moving forward and found myself entering an immense void, completely dark, infinite in size, yet also infinitely comforting. Pitch-black as it was, it was also brimming over with light: a light that seemed to come from a brilliant orb that I now sensed near me. The orb was a kind of "interpreter" between me and this vast presence surrounding me. It was as if I were being born into a larger world, and the universe itself was like a giant cosmic womb, and the orb (which I sensed was somehow connected with, or even identical to, the woman on the butterfly wing) was guiding me through it.

Worksheet Letting Go or Holding Tight – The Right to Die

Tasks:

1. List the facts known about Tony Nicklinson and his wish.
2. What is the Twitter campaign all about? What might be Mr. Nicklinson's reasons to send his tweet?
3. Answer the survey question "Should the right to die be enshrined[6] in law?"
   Discuss with your neighbour how you would decide in Tony Nicklinson's case. Give reasons. Present your arguments to the class.
4. Do research on the outcome of Tony Nicklinson's case and present it to the class.
5. Do research on Stephen Hawking. Present him and his way of dealing with his illness.

Text: Twitter Campaign Over Right-To-Die Case

Mark White, Sky News, 19 June 2012

A paralysed man who heads to the High Court today to seek the right to die is at the centre of an extraordinary social media campaign to persuade him to change his mind.

Less than a week after Wiltshire father Tony Nicklinson posted his first comments on Twitter, many thousands of people from around the world are following his plight on the micro-blogging site.

The 58-year-old suffers from "locked-in syndrome" since a severe stroke seven years ago and can communicate only by moving his eyelids. Mr Nicklinson argues that his life is "dull, miserable, demeaning, undignified and intolerable" and is seeking legal protection for any doctor who helps him end his life.

Since Nicklinson's signalling his determination to die and seeking comments on Twitter, strangers have bombarded him with pro-life messages.

Many others have expressed support for the father of two grown daughters, from Melksham. In March, he won the right to take his case to the High Court and is seeking to make legal history by challenging the Government over the right to die.

On June 13 he posted his first tweet: "Hello world. I am tony nicklinson. I have locked-in syndrome and this is my first ever tweet." He communicates through a specially-adapted computer which records blinks and tiny head movements.

Within hours he received many replies of sympathy and support. But others urged him to change his mind. One wrote: "I do believe in miracles and will pray for you. God will heal you one day. God bless you, He loves you so very much." Another wrote: "I would hate to see you depart from this world without fully exploring all you can do."

In response, Mr Nicklinson has said: "People want to know if I will change my mind because of Twitter. Let's hear the judgement first and maybe I'll tell you."

---

[6] to be enshrined in law: to be stated in a legal document, to be made a law

Some campaign groups have expressed concern at the outspoken nature of some of the comments. A spokesman for Dignity in Dying said they hoped Twitter users would be respectful of Mr Nicklinson, even if they do not agree with him.

Tony Nicklinson's wife Jane said he had no intention of changing his mind.

Before today's hearing he issued a statement saying: "I'm delighted that the issues surrounding assisted dying are to be aired in court. I need help in almost every aspect of my life. I cannot scratch if I itch, I cannot pick my nose if it is blocked and I can only eat if I am fed like a baby – only I won't grow out of it, unlike the baby."

His legal action claims to seek a court declaration that a doctor could intervene to end his life and have a common law defence of "necessity". The case differs to previous attempts to amend the law on assisted suicide, like the case of multiple sclerosis sufferer Debbie Purdy, who won a clarification of prosecution policy where someone assists a terminally-ill person to die.

Mr. Nicklinson's paralysis is so severe that he cannot simply be assisted to take his own life and he would have to be killed by someone.

Earlier this year, an independent commission on assisted dying concluded for the first time that certain people should be helped to die. But this applies only to those who are terminally ill and are able to take the final action to end their lives themselves – which excludes Mr. Nicklinson.

Vote: **Should the right to die be enshrined by law?**
(The Telegraph, UK, June 21, 2012)

NO, the right to life should always take precedence.
YES, it is cruel to keep people alive when they no longer want to live.

Results: 88 percent NO
12 percent YES

For the teacher:

ad 4:
On 16 August 2012, Tony Nicklinson's request was turned down by the High Court of Justice. On learning the outcome of his appeal, he refused to eat. When he contracted pneumonia he deteriorated rapidly and died on 22 August 2012.

While-reading Activities IV

Worksheet Letting Go or Holding Tight – Gambling with DEATH

Tasks:

1. How is Granny Weatherwax's visitor presented?
2. How do Granny and her visitor interact? Which attitude prevails in this story?
3. Sum up this extract in a few sentences.
4. Do research on Terry Pratchett's attitude towards dying.

Extract: Granny has a visitor

Terry Pratchett, **Maskerade**, 1995

DEATH comes to Granny Weatherwax. The old witch is protecting a baby.

Granny breathed out, slowly.

'Come and sit where I can see you. That's good manners. And let me tell you right now that I ain't at all afraid of you.'

The tall, black-robed figure walked across the floor and sat down on a handy barrel, leaning its scythe against the wall. Then it pushed back its hood.

Granny folded her arms and stared calmly at the visitor, meeting his gaze eye-to-socket.

I AM IMPRESSED.

'I have faith.'

REALLY? IN WHAT PARTICULAR DEITY?

'Oh, none of *them*.'

THEN FAITH IN WHAT?

'Just faith, you know. In general.'

Death leaned forward. The candlelight raised new shadows on his skull.

COURAGE IS EASY BY CANDLELIGHT. YOUR FAITH, I SUSPECT, IS IN THE FLAME.

Death grinned.

Granny leaned forward, and blew out the candle. Then she folded her arms again and stared fiercely ahead of her.

After some length of time a voice said, ALL RIGHT, YOU'VE MADE YOUR POINT.

Granny lit a match. Its flare illuminated the skull opposite, which hadn't moved.

'Fair enough,' she said, as she relit the candle. 'We don't want to be sitting here all night, do we? How many have you come for?'

ONE.

'The cow?'

Death shook his head.

'It could *be* the cow.'

NO. THAT WOULD BE CHANGING HISTORY.

'History is about things changing.'

NO.

Granny sat back.

'Then I challenge you to a game. That's traditional. That's *allowed*.'

Death was silent for a moment.

THIS IS TRUE.

'Good.'

CHALLENGING ME BY MEANS OF A GAME IS ALLOWABLE.

'Yes.'

HOWEVER … YOU UNDERSTAND THAT TO WIN ALL YOU MUST GAMBLE ALL?

'Double or quits? Yes, I know.'

BUT NOT CHESS.

'Can't abide chess.'

OR CRIPPLE MR ONION. I'VE NEVER BEEN ABLE TO UNDERSTAND THE RULES.

'Very well. How about one hand of poker? Five cards each, no draws? Sudden death, as they say.'

Death thought about this, too. YOU KNOW THIS FAMILY?

'No.'

THEN WHY?

'Are we talking or are we playing?'

OH, VERY WELL.

Granny picked up the pack of cards and shuffled it, not looking at her hands, and smiling at Death all the time. She dealt five cards each, and reached down …

A bony hand grasped hers. BUT FIRST, MISTRESS WEATHERWAX – WE WILL EXCHANGE CARDS.

He picked up the two piles and transposed them, and then nodded at Granny.

MADAM?

Granny looked at her cards, and threw them down.

FOUR QUEENS. HMM. THAT *IS* VERY HIGH.

Death looked down at his cards, and then up into Granny's steady, blue-eyed gaze.

Neither moved for some time.

Then Death laid the hand on the table. I LOSE, he said, ALL I HAVE IS FOUR ONES.

He looked back into Granny's eyes for a moment. There was a blue glow in the depth of his eye-sockets. Maybe, for the merest fraction of a second, barely noticeable even to the closest observation, one winked off.

Granny nodded, and extended a hand.

She prided herself on the ability to judge people by their gaze and their handshake, which in this case was a rather chilly one.

'Take the cow,' she said.

IT IS A VALUABLE CREATURE.

'Who knows what the child will become?'

Death stood up, and reached for his scythe.

He said, ow.

'Ah, yes. I couldn't help noticing,' said Granny Weatherwax, as the tension drained out of the atmosphere, 'that you seem to be sparing that arm.'

OH, YOU KNOW HOW IT IS. REPETITIVE ACTIONS AND SO ON …

'It could get serious if you left it.'

HOW SERIOUS?

'Want me to have a look?'

WOULD YOU MIND? IT CERTAINLY ACHES ON COLD NIGHTS.

Granny stood up and reached out, but her hands went straight through.

'Look, you're going to have to make yourself a bit more solid if I'm to do anything –'

POSSIBLY A BOTTLE OF SUCKROSE AND AKWA?

'Sugar and water? I expect you know that's only for the hard of thinking. Come on, roll up that sleeve. Don't be a big baby. What's the worst I can do to you?'

Granny's hands touched smooth bone. She'd felt worse. At least these had never had flesh on them.

She felt, thought, gripped, twisted …

There was a click.

OW.

'Now try it above the shoulder.'

ER. HMM. YES. IT DOES SEEM CONSIDERABLY MORE FREE. YES, INDEED. MY WORD, YES. THANK YOU VERY MUCH.

'If it gives you trouble again, you know where I live.'

THANK YOU. THANK YOU VERY MUCH.

'You know where everyone lives. Tuesday morning is a good time. I'm generally in.'

I SHALL REMEMBER. THANK YOU.

'By appointment, in your case. No offence meant.'

THANK YOU.

Death walked away. A moment later there was a faint gasp from the cow. That and a slight sagging of the skin were all that apparently marked the transition from living animal to cooling meat.

Granny picked up the baby and laid a hand on its forehead. 'Fever's gone,' she said.

MISTRESS WEATHERWAX? said Death from the doorway.

'Yes, sir?'

I HAVE TO KNOW. WHAT WOULD HAVE HAPPENED IF I HAD NOT … LOST?

'At the cards, you mean?'

YES. WHAT WOULD YOU HAVE DONE?

Granny laid the baby down carefully on the straw, and smiled.

'Well,' she said, 'for a start … I'd have broken your bloody arm.'

For the teacher:

ad 4:

Terry Pratchett, born in 1948, is one of Britain's most popular writers. His Discworld novels are read in many languages and popular all over the world. They often include literary, historical and scientific topics and mythological references without being school-marmy. Terry Pratchett is not only a keen science fiction author but a humanist and environmentalist. He co-wrote books like *The Science of Discworld.* He also published a large number of books for children, in which he tackles issues such as xenophobia, discrimination and the British class system, but again, as in his novels for adults, his humanitarian aims are presented without overshadowing his extremely witty and meaningful writing and very likeable characters.

In his latest novels, co-written with the author Stephen Baxter, *The Long Earth* (2012) and *The Long War* (2013) he deals with colonisation and globalisation and perceived and actual threats by others.

When he was diagnosed with Alzheimer's in late 2007, he stated in interviews that he would not want to continue living in a dehumanised state but commit suicide before that happened. Extracts can be found on *youtube*.

Among other publications and interviews, there is a two-part programme with and about him *Living with Alzheimer's* published by the BBC in 2008, *Shaking Hands with Death* in 2010, and the 2011 documentary *Terry Pratchett: Choosing to Die,* in which he explains assisted death.

While-reading Activities IV

Worksheet Letting Go or Holding Tight – From Beyond the Grave

Tasks:

1. Sum up this extract in a few sentences.
2. What do you think of "interactive gravestones"?
3. Discuss with your neighbour what you would want to be remembered by. Make a list and present it to the class.
4. Create a piece which you would like to find on your interactive gravestone.

Extract: **Interactive gravestones link to online tales of life**
Li-mei Hoang, Reuters, 6 September 2012

London – Summing up the life of a dearly beloved departed relative with just a terse description etched in stone may become a thing of the past with the introduction of interactive codes on gravestones.

One funeral company in the southern English town of Poole is offering to add quick response (QR) codes to headstones which will link smartphones to online memorials illustrated with pictures, videos and contributions from family and friends.

Chester Pearce funeral directors said QR barcodes enable visitors to learn a lot more about the person buried beneath gravestones than the age, dates of birth and death and the odd biblical passage or literary quote usually written on them.

"It's about keeping people's memories alive in different ways," managing director Stephen Nimmo told Reuters. "When you lose somebody, whether it be suddenly or ongoing, you can really struggle with things. Talking about them is very important, keeping their memory going is very important and this is just an add-on to that."

Gill Tuttiet, 53, was one of the first customers in Poole to use the technology for her late husband Timothy. "Tim was quite outward-going and game for anything. I think this is the way forward and Tim would have wanted that."

"We've all got a story to tell," Nimmo said.

While-reading Activities IV

Worksheet Letting Go or Holding Tight – Keeping Memories Alive

Tasks:

1. Before you read the explanations, describe the photos and their impact on you.
2. Discuss in groups whether you think the upkeep of these graves (a hundred years after WW I) is important or whether the places should be returned to nature.

All tombstones are the same size. Officers and enlisted soldiers are honoured in the same way in this military graveyard near Ypres.

These memorial tributes were placed at the Menin Gate Memorial in Ypres, where each evening at 8 o'clock a group of musicians play *The Last Post* and groups of adults and children from Britain, the USA, Canada, and Australia lay down wreaths and remember their dead and missing of World War One.

This war cemetery near Langemark in Flanders, Belgium, is the last resting place of 44,081 German soldiers. In the background, four statues and houses of the village Langemark can be seen.

This idyllic lake was created by an underground explosion which blew up German soldiers in their underground shelter on Hill 60 near Ypres. The crater filled with water. There is no plaque remembering their deaths. In summer local young people have parties here.

Task 1:

Find out more about the battles around Hill 60 near Zillebeke, the high ground of which was held by German soldiers, the slopes by French, English, Canadian and Australian troops.

Task 2:

Discuss which arguments you would present to the Volksbund Deutsche Kriegsgräberfürsorge to make sure that the German soldiers on Hill 60 are remembered, too.

Answers to the Questions for Consideration

In the following, summaries of the answers to the questions in the students' book can be found.

Questions for Consideration I – August 2026: There Will Come Soft Rains
by Ray Bradbury

The story is, as the speaking clock announces, set in 2026. The sophisticated, highly mechanised house is fully automated and keeps running even though the people living in the house have been wiped out by an atomic blast.

The house runs along its programmed routine, but it is not "intelligent": It has not realised that its inhabitants no longer exist and that neither watering the lawn nor cooking are necessary.

The simple rhymes, which sound like nursery rhymes, are a contrast to the modern house but also show the house's simplicity and/or the programmer's childlike mind.

The poem, which is randomly selected for the evening recital, reminds mankind that it is not needed and that nature – even after total destruction – will reclaim the place. The recital probably sounds soothing and optimistic, but its message predicts the ending of the story. The ongoing reading of the poem in the final passage counterpoints the house's destruction. Its message becomes totally clear when, on the following morning, from amidst the rubble of the house the speaking clock repeatedly announces a new day: nature will reclaim the ground and life will go on without human beings.

Questions for Consideration II – The Machine Stops by E. M. Forster

In this future world, people live in underground cells of their own which are "run" by the Machine. People interact via screens and social network-style media. Touching others is considered obscene. People must apply to become parents; their children are educated in nurseries while the adults return to their individual cells.

Vashti, who is ghostly white and so big and flabby that she can hardly move, does not care to leave her cell and complains when her son Kuno summons her to his place on the other side of the world. People are not interested in seeing new places and in making new discoveries, therefore the windows of the airships, which are rarely used anyway, are shuttered and old ideas are recycled and repeated.

The Machine, which is revered as a God, and its manual considered as the Bible, have taken on Christian values.

Kuno has always been suspicious of the Machine. That is one of the reasons why he was not granted permission to become a father. When he notices very early that the Machine does not run smoothly any more, his mother does not believe him. She believes in the Machine's infallibility and does not trust Kuno's words or her own perception. When the faults become obvious people start complaining to the repair mechanism, which is faulty too. They get used to the air not being pure any more, to the dim lights and to the beds no longer appearing. They have resigned themselves to this life as they do not know any other. The Machine and the people depending on it will be completely destroyed when failing airships crash into the landing shafts and the underground world implodes. Only the lawless, those who have been expelled by the Machine to die on the 'inhabitable' earth above ground, will survive.

Questions for Consideration III – Musée des Beaux Arts by W. H. Auden

The Old Masters, the painters of the Renaissance, understood human suffering and its place in life – which is that even when a tragedy occurs or a holy event takes place, people go on doing banal tasks and living their own petty lives. They are indifferent and do not care.

In the first part of the poem, the birth and death of Christ – who, for believers, is the Saviour of the world – is not even noticed by most of the bystanders. And in the second part of the poem, Icarus' miraculous flight is not considered a spectacular event. His fall from the sky is just noticed as a splash by the ploughman who does not even turn around, and it is not considered important by the ship's crew either. Miracles do not count. Everyday life goes on.

People are not very much interested in what goes on elsewhere, outside their own sphere of interest and influence. Patriots and freedom fighters from all over Europe felt drawn to fight in the Spanish Civil War (George Orwell among them), but very soon World War II captured the general interest. People disappeared, the population was suppressed, but the Spanish dictatorship persisted well into the 1950s, without much outcry in the Western world.

Auden takes the paintings as a starting point for his musings and reflections. It is not his intention to give an accurate description. The dying of human beings is not considered as important or spectacular in his poem. In Sara Teasdale's poem, nature wins after human destruction. People and their dying will be forgotten.

Questions for Consideration IV – Landscape with the Fall of Icarus
by William Carlos Williams

In his poem, William Carlos Williams comments on the same Brueghel picture as W. H. Auden. He describes the picture in clear and precise language, which is very modernist, being without punctuation. Instead of expressing the message of the picture in words, as W. H. Auden did, he does it by relegating Icarus's name to the last line, thus turning it into a banal event not registered by anybody. Before that he describes the reason for his fall with clinical precision, as one would a lab experiment. He does not mention the ship specifically; the "edge of the sea" and "the event off the coast" convey all that is worth knowing about the setting.

Questions for Consideration V – Stop All the Clocks by W.H. Auden

The very simple rhyme scheme of the poem – aa bb – is repetitive and makes it solemn. The poem expresses melancholy and inconsolable grief. The writer goes so far as to request the stopping of all clocks, even the dismantling of the celestial bodies and the emptying of oceans; which is of course totally unrealistic because the Earth and the other celestial bodies will continue their course, and time will go on.

We are shaken out of the mood of total unhappiness by a fifth and last stanza which W.H. Auden had included in the 1936 version of the poem which was sung in music halls. Here, the beloved departed is driven to the cemetery by a racing motor hearse driver at breakneck speed and the solemn melancholy atmosphere dissolves in a chuckle.

Questions for Consideration VI – Night Funeral in Harlem by Langston Hughes

The speaker in this poem observes a lavish funeral with expensive fine cars, probably to transport the coffin and the chief mourners, a coffin lined with satin, a wreath of flowers and a preacher who is paid for his service by the deceased man's girl-friend.

We realise that the speaker, as well as the deceased man, are poor. But the funeral is conducted in state. The organ plays, the coffin is closed and carried to the hearse by six pall bearers, then driven to the cemetery.

And when the hearse disappears round the corner, it occurs to the observant speaker that the feelings of the mourners are far more important than the money spent on a good sending-away. The mourners' tears count.

This quiet and reflective mood cannot be compared to the all-out grief in Auden's Stop All the Clocks. Its mourner wants to stop the world for all to see that he has lost the centre of his life.

Questions for Consideration VII – Alabanza: In Praise of Local 100 by Martin Espada

The beginning of this poem describes the people who worked (and died in the 9/11 attacks) in the café on the 10th floor of the North Tower. Their idiosyncrasies are mentioned and characterise them, for example their tattoos, their clothing, their background. The descriptive mood evokes the images of immigrants working in this place in a very personal way.

The poem is a eulogy praising these immigrants from Ecuador, Yemen, Mexico, Haiti, Ghana, Bangladesh and the Dominican Republic. The poet mentions the Spanish name *Republica Dominicana* – probably to indicate that the immigrants did not use English as their main language.

We notice the religious imagery in references to the plague of the frogs, the light, the candle, the altar of cans, even mysticism in the worship of the dark saint of the seas.

Alabanza – Praise – is repeated all through the poem in Spanish and in English. It resembles an invocation or a prayer. We hear the chant of different nations; we hear the radio and the waitress singing, until noises louder than thunder and destruction, like bursting dams, break into the kitchen and destroy the immigrants' harmonious work life. Their charred remains are thrust into the air. Their community, their "civilisation" is dead, like Atlantis.

The religious overtone becomes doubtful. Do the souls of the departed meet God? God has no face. But still the writer continues to say *Alabanza*. He praises the immigrants who worked together, who mingled and bore no hatred towards others, even when their states were locked in war.

The poem ends on a peaceful and comforting note. The dead unite – Afghans and Spanish-speaking people sing and dance together. This gives hope for the living.

Questions for Consideration VIII – The Scarlet Ibis by James Hurst

This story is set between summer and autumn. The ibis, exotic and out of its place, falls out of a tree, dead, thus foreshadowing tragic events.

Being different and ways of dealing with otherness are the main topics of the short story. We notice this when the narrator's handicapped little brother is introduced.

The boy is called Doodle. As soon as the narrator starts talking about his younger brother, we notice that he acts in his own interest when he teaches his handicapped brother to walk: He does not want a brother who is different. He looks after him, he pulls him around in a go-cart, but he also bullies him into learning to walk and to swim. The narrator mentions his pride which turned into a matter of life and death, his pride whose slave he was. We realise this when the narrator pushes Doodle to continue. Even though the little boy has no force left he urges him on with the words "Aw, come on, Doodle, you can do it. Do you want to be different from everybody else when you start school?" He counters Doodle's soft answering question "Does it make any difference?" saying "It certainly does" and shows that he cannot accept his brother with his imperfections.

On the one hand, the narrator acts as his brother's keeper when he supervises him and pulls him around. But when he does not heed Doodle's shouts "Brother, Brother, don't leave me!" because he is disappointed with him, he turns into the biblical Cain. The narrator leaves Doodle behind in a thunderstorm – though he knows that being left is his brother's biggest fear. He cruelly neglects him and indirectly kills him.

Cain, who has slain his brother Aaron in a fit of rage, says to God that he cannot be made accountable for his brother's well-being. He asks: Am I to be my brother's keeper? (Gen. 4:9)
This is in stark contrast with the biblical message of brotherly love and charity.

In the end, the narrator holds his dead brother, weeping and bemoaning his death.

How to Continue

What do you think: is writing obituaries morbid? A taboo topic?

As we have already seen with interactive tombstones, with online sites for mourning and remembering loved ones, a person's life and appreciation do not stop when the person dies. Obituaries reflect on what made a person special, what made the person unique, where their qualities lay, but also which difficulties they coped with and how they lived their life.

In an obituary writing project, students learn what to emphasise, how to research carefully and how to present facts honestly in order to value and appreciate a person's life.

Some might consider writing obituaries morbid because talking of death, especially of one's own death, is still considered a taboo topic. But why not use famous people? We all know that drawers in newspapers' offices and files in news agencies are full with skeleton obituaries of important men and women and are updated regularly.

Students can refer to the text on page 75 and write obituaries for their pets. Or they can remember Roger Ebert with the material on page 76 and the hints and rules on pages 72 and 74.

We can then continue and ask the students what they would like to be remembered for. They can write lists, short texts, poems, songs and also include pictures or little films as material for an interactive tombstone.

A test, which is a mediation task of a German obituary remembering Wolfgang Herrndorf's death in August 2013, can be done at the end of the unit.

The inspirational quotes and their relevance for people in mourning will give food for thought and discussion. Are they really uplifting? Or rather a nuisance? Do you read the posts people state on their social networking sites? Do you see meaning in the little poems in the announcements of death in the papers?

With these questions in mind, the class can conclude this unit on death with a collection of sayings, poems and songs they find comforting and meaningful.

Post-reading Activities

Creative Obituary Projects

Kerry O'Neill, eHow Contributor

Teachers can use obituaries for creative project ideas.

Many people, at one time or another, have thought about their own death. Although it is a morbid topic, an obituary can be quite fascinating. Encapsulating a life in a mere paragraph presents itself as a challenge. Through development of creative projects, teachers can use obituaries to enhance the writing skills of their students.

Character Obituary

The characters from literature can serve as inspirations for obituaries. Assign students a character from a piece of literature. Using the story in which the character appears, students write an obituary for the person. Students should consider their accomplishments, who they have survived and what type of person they were. Teachers can choose characters that have already died, or they can select characters who are living and determine what type of death makes sense for them. Have students share their obituaries with the class.

Guess Who

The students can all write an obituary for characters they have studied in the class. Provide about fifteen to twenty minutes for the students to write the obituary, leaving off the name of the character. Then have students come to the front of the class and read their obituaries. The students guess whom the obituary describes. Use this opportunity for class discussion as well. Was the character accurately described? Was there anything missing?

Historical Obituary

Select a list of historical figures. This can correlate to a theme, such as the Roaring Twenties or Black History Month. The teacher can also select a wide variety of figures. Assign students a figure and ask them to research this person. Students will then write their obituaries. When possible, present the actual obituary for the character to compare and contrast. Use the activity to facilitate class discussion about the famous figures.

Personal Obituary

Students should consider their own personal goals and possible achievements. Have students write their own obituaries. Set very specific guidelines. Have the students omit the cause of death and details surrounding it. Have them focus on their own accomplishments and activities. Stress to the students that an obituary celebrates people's lives. The activity allows students to ponder the paths they will take in life and the achievements they hope to accomplish.

Bear in mind: A well-written obituary is an important tribute to a person's unique life.

Find additional information at: www.ehow.com/info_7949307_creative-obituary-projects.html

Post-reading Activities

Worksheet A 'Must-Read' Obituary

Tasks:

1. Why did the obituary for Mary A. "Pink" Mullaney make national headlines?
2. What do you think of the family's way of sharing Mary Mullaney's nuggets of wisdom?
3. Read Mullaney's obituary in full at:
   http://www.feerickfuneralhome.com/notices.php?id=1036

Extract: Wisconsin Woman's Awe-Inspiring Obituary a 'Must Read'

Katie Kindelan, ABC News, 11 September 2013

"If you're about to throw away an old pair of pantyhose, stop" is not the way most obituaries begin, but, then, according to her family, Mary A. "Pink" Mullaney was no ordinary woman.

The Wisconsite died on Sunday, Sept. 1, at the age of 85, leaving behind six children and 17 grandchildren who adored her so much they crafted an obituary so heartfelt and touching that it made national headlines.

The obituary's opening line stems from one of Mullaney's most well-known maxims: Never throw away old pantyhose.

"Use the old ones for rosary repairs, to tie the gutter, childproof the cabinets, tie up the toilet flapper or hang Christmas ornaments," reads the obituary, written by seven or eight of Mullaney's children and grandchildren who gathered together in their hometown of Milwaukee after her death.

"We wanted to portray who she was and her love for people and just her funny ways of going about it," one of her sons said. "She was an extraordinary person in an ordinary way. Survived by so and so and accomplished this and that didn't capture that."

Mullaney, a devout Catholic who volunteered in a nursing home and delivered Communion up until age 81, also had kind and gentle rules surrounding the rituals of her faith.

"I see her as the hands and feet of Jesus," said her son. "What she taught all of us is to love others as Christ loved us."

Worksheet Obituary Writing

Tasks:

1. Write an obituary for a person of your choice, following the rules below.
2. Do the same for a character in a novel, for example Effing in Paul Auster's **Moon Palace**. Compare your obituaries, and point out similarities and differences.
3. Sum up the extract on page 75. Discuss why people might want obituaries for their pets.
4. Write an obituary for your pet or for a friend's pet.

How to Write a Simple Obituary

By Chelsea Fithgerald eHow Contributor

Obituaries are printed in newspapers and other publications to notify the public of a death. Certain guidelines are necessary to include all the pertinent information in a simple obituary.

1. If possible, talk to a close relative of the deceased person to gather your information. Confirm the name spelling, names of relatives, dates and other important information with a second source, especially if the first person you spoke with was emotionally distraught. When people are upset and grieving, they may forget important details or make errors in spelling or dates.

2. Document the dates of the person's birth and death, and the location of both.

3. List the person's children, grandchildren, parents and siblings, and indicate whether they are deceased or alive.

4. Write down any interesting facts about the person. If the deceased received a military award or work honor, served as head of an organization or was active in religious or social committees, mention those details. You can also include the age at death, number of grandchildren and other pertinent facts that celebrate the deceased's life and what was important to him.

5. Include the funeral and viewing times, dates and locations for anybody who is not in contact with the relatives, but would like to drop by and pay respect.

6. Contact family members to find out if they want a charitable organization or group to receive donations in lieu of sending flowers or plants. For instance, if the person died of a rare disease, the family may desire that contributions be sent to the foundation, or if the person was an avid reader, to a library.

7. Proofread the obituary once you complete it; if time allows, read it again a few hours or a day later to catch any spelling, grammar or punctuation errors or incorrect facts. If time is short, ask another person to proofread it for you. Often, once you write something, your brain may skip over a misspelled word or other error without really seeing it. Reading it aloud is another effective way to catch errors.

Tips & Warnings

- It is appropriate to include the person's philosophy of life, or a particular quote or Bible verse that guided his life.
- Never put the deceased person's home address in an obituary. There are individuals who prey on these homes since they know the family will be attending the viewing[7] and funeral.

Extract: Something new for Singapore's pampered pets – obituaries

Kevin Lim, Reuters, 11 December 2012

Grieving pet owners in Singapore, known for lavishing care in life on their animals, can soon share their feelings about furred family members after they pad off to the great beyond – via obituaries in the city-state's largest newspaper.

From Sunday, The Straits Times pet section will let pet owners publish goodbye messages to their favourite non-human companions along with an accompanying photo.

The memorials will be part of a "pets' corner" in the paper's classifieds[8] section.

The decision to market obituaries to pet owners in tiny Singapore, one of the world's richest countries in terms of per capita income, comes as wealthy Asians have fewer kids and shower more attention on pets.

Research firm Euromonitor, in a recent report on Singapore's pet care market, said people are spending more on premium pet food as well as accessories such as designer pet clothing.

"Many pet owners are increasingly treating their pets as household members and are therefore pampering their pets with luxurious food, products and services, just as they would dote on their family," it said.

Needless to say, the obituaries are not free – they will each run S$50 ($40,96), with a goods and services tax of 7 percent on top of that.

---

[7] public viewing: hours during which friends and relatives of a deceased person can come to the funeral home, a church or a chapel and "view" the deceased, either in an open casket or a closed one. Attending a wake (= public viewing) is a social event and considered an important part of the grieving process as a chance of a personal goodbye.
Mentioned in passing: "Going to a public viewing" means "attending a wake". Perhaps we can now understand the surprised looks of our British friends when Germans use it in connection with football.

[8] classifieds = classified ads = classified advertisements

Post-reading Activities

Worksheet Obituary Writing – Remembering Roger Ebert

Tasks:

1. In these tributes to Roger Ebert, underline the most important phrases and statements.
2. Use them to write an obituary for Roger Ebert. Pretend you are a Hollywood director or actor.

In Memoriam Rober Ebert 1942–2013

Hollywood Directors Remember 'Legend' Roger Ebert

Roger Ebert influenced generations of film critics and helped millions of movie fans discover films they might not otherwise have seen. But Ebert is also a hero to directors, who saw in him a champion with the clout to rescue movies from obscurity, make pointed criticisms or spread his passionate appreciation far and wide.

Danny Boyle:
For me, the great thing about coming here to America and releasing films is that this nation is obsessed with movies. Despite all the comings and goings in papers and blogs, people are obsessed with movies the way filmmakers are obsessed with them. And Roger was a great inspiration like that, and a great man. He loved film, and he remained so right until the end.

Paul Weitz:
I read Ebert's 'Great Films' books for inspiration. He wasn't part of the pack, wasn't trying to be friends with the cool kids. He helped navigate a transitional period of film history in which a good film might have a budget of a hundred million or a hundred thousand dollars.

Michael Moore:
Roger Ebert was the champion of the underdog filmmaker. Early on, he told middle America about Spike Lee and Errol Morris and Ang Lee and myself and so many others. He gave as much attention to an obscure but brilliant foreign film as he did to a Hollywood blockbuster. He was a fierce advocate for art and free speech and for stamping out the ignorance that seems at times to be the lifeblood of this country. He answered only to himself and if you made a good movie he wasn't going to shut up until everyone saw it. He even started a film festival in the Illinois town where he went to college called The Roger Ebert Overlooked Film Festival – for movies that didn't get proper distribution but were brilliant.

Over a decade ago, before he got cancer, he sent me a personal letter about how he was going to lose weight and get healthy – and told me I should join him. I eventually did, and I began the long, slow road to a better self. He lost something like a hundred pounds and never felt better. And then cancer struck.

Steven Spielberg:
Roger loved movies. They were his life. His reviews went far deeper than simply thumbs up or thumbs down. He wrote with passion through a real knowledge of film and film history, and in doing so, helped many movies find their audiences. And he put television ciriticism on the map.

Martin Sorcese:
The death of Roger Ebert is an incalculable loss for movie culture and for film criticism.

Test

Mediation Wolfgang Herrndorf and his Exit

Content:	10 credits
Language:	15 credits
Total:	**25 credits**

Task:

Transform this German obituary in an obituary for an English literary magazine.

Schreiben, als ob dies das wahre Leben sei

Nachruf Wolfgang Herrndorf, der Autor des Erfolgsromans „Tschick“, ist mit 48 Jahren gestorben.
Thomas Klingenmaier, Stuttgarter Zeitung, 28. 08. 2013

Am besten wagt man mal was. „Die Straße verlor sich kurz hinter dem verlassenen Dorf, und wir mussten querfeldein“, erklärt der Bürgersohn Maik, der Erzähler in Wolfgang Herrndorfs Roman „Tschick“, seine Route. Querfeldein, das war auch der Kurs des Autors Herrndorf: weg vom Vornehmen und Braven, aber auch weg von allem, was nach angestrengter Avantgarde aussieht. Weg vor allem von der miefigen Humorlosigkeit und pedantischen Verbasteltheit, die hierzulande gerne als Literatur angesehen wird. Herrndorf schrieb wie junge Katzen mit Wollknäueln kämpfen: als sei ein schöneres Spiel gar nicht vorstellbar, als sei das Leben genau dazu da.

Herrndorf, Jahrgang 1965, war kein Karriereliterat, sondern eigentlich Maler. Zuerst aufgefallen ist er als Mitarbeiter des Satiremagazins „Titanic“. Man hat das seinen Texten angemerkt. Sich ein Bild von der Welt zu machen, das heißt für den Karikaturisten auch, die verborgene Komik sichtbar zu machen. Zugleich musste Herrndorf niemanden mehr in die Pfanne hauen, das hätte er ja jederzeit mit einem einzigen Bild erledigen können.

Sein Debütroman „In Plüschgewittern“ erschien 2002, aber sein Durchbruch kam 2010 mit „Tschick“. Diese Geschichte zweier junger Burschen aus sehr unterschiedlichen Verhältnissen ist zu Recht als modernes Spiel mit der Freundschaft von Tom Sawyer und Huckleberry Finn gelobt worden. Aber solche Vergleiche bringen die Gefahr mit sich, jemanden wegzusortieren im Museum der Literaturmotive und -heroen: Du darfst neben Mark Twain stehen, aber sei schön still.

Herrndorf wollte alles andere als still sein, er wollte einen Sound, er wollte Texte, die man sich laut vorlas, weil man neugierig war, wie sie klangen. Er näherte sich der Umgangssprache, aber nie straßenprotzig. Er konnte das Banale beschreiben, ohne es zu veräppeln, ohne sich in Wonnen der Gewöhnlichkeit zu suhlen oder das kleine Munkeln zu überhöhen.
Hier wollen Maik und sein Kumpel Benzin schläucheln: „Problem war natürlich, dass wir keinen Schlauch hatten. Wir suchten zuerst das Gelände hinter der Tankstelle ab, dann das Unterholz, dann einen Acker, dann immer weiter weg. Wir fanden Radkappen, Plastikplanen, Pfandflaschen, Unmengen Bierdosen und am Ende sogar einen Fünf-Liter-Kanister ohne Verschluss, aber irgendwas Schlauchähnliches fanden wir nicht.“ So macht man aus dem Wühlen im Dreck Musik.

Wie virtuos und vergnügt Herrndorf mit Erwartungen, Genremustern und Sprache umgehen konnte fällt besondern auf, wenn man gleich nach „Tschick“ den 2011 erschienenen Roman „Sand“ liest, den direkten Nachfolger – ganz anders, aber genauso vital. Ein Abenteuerroman und ein Krimi ist das, spielt 1972 in Nordafrika und greift Themen wie Terror und Geheimpolitik auf. Aber Herrndorf macht das habituelle

Lügen von Profiintriganten zum schon wieder subversiv komischen Konstruktionsprinzip einer manchmal gruseligen Erzählwelt: Hier soll manchmal eine Wahrheit aus Figuren herausgefoltert werden, die dann doch nur wieder mit aller Kraft in Zweifel gezogen werden müsste.

Zu diesem Zeitpunkt schrieb Herrndorf längst sehr offen über extrem Privates. Ein bösartiger Hirntumor war bei ihm diagnostiziert worden, seit 2010 beschrieb er im Internet sein Leben mit der Krankheit zum Tode: Dieses Blog ist ein weiteres Großwerk von ihm. Gestern war für Wolfgang Herrndorf das Ende des Weges erreicht, und „Sand“ ist auch ein Buch der Wut über die Wegnahme von Chancen und den Raub von Leben. Was für eine großartige Sache das ist, für eine Weile auf Erden zu sein, auch wenn die momentan ein Sauladen ist, das hat Wolfgang Herrndorf einnehmend beschrieben.

* * *

This is how Wolfgang Herrndorf ended his blog:

ARBEIT UND STRUKTUR

ARCHIV IMPRESSUM

Wolfgang Herrndorf

Schluss

Wolfgang Herrndorf hat sich am Montag, den 26. August 2013 gegen 23.15 Uhr am Ufer des Hohenzollernkanals erschossen.

You can find this and older posts at www.wolfgang-herrndorf.de

Post-reading Activities

Worksheet Inspirational Thoughts

Tasks:

1. A lot of inspirational thoughts are posted on websites. Discuss with your neighbour if you read them, if you post them and what you think of them.
2. Rephrase the quotes below in your own words.
3. Talk about the one you like best. Explain why you chose it and why it made an impression on you.
4. Share your own favourite quote with the others. Or explain why you don't have one.

1. *You can cut all the flowers but you cannot keep spring from coming.* (Pablo Neruda)

2. *Your life has purpose.*
Your story is important.
Your dreams count.
Your voice matters.
You were born to make an impact.

3. *Wake up every morning with the thought that something wonderful is about to happen.*

4. *The world is indeed full of peril and in it there are many dark places. But still there is much that is fair. And though in all lands, love is now mingled with grief, it still grows, perhaps, the greater.* (J.R.R. Tolkien, *The Lord of the Rings)*

5. *I believe that imagination is stronger than knowledge. That myth is more potent than history. That dreams are more powerful than facts. That hope always triumphs over experience. That laughter is the only cure for grief. And I believe that love is stronger than death.* (Robert Fulghum)

6. *In a world filled with hate, we must still dare to hope. In a world filled with anger, we must still dare to comfort. In a world filled with despair, we must still dare to dream. And in a world filled with distrust, we must still dare to believe.* (Michael Jackson)

When you're standing on the crossroads
That you cannot comprehend
Just remember that death is not the end
And all your dreams have vanished
And you don't know what's up the bend
Just remember that death is not the end
Not the end, not the end.
(Nick Cave)

* * *

Task:

Describe the headstone in the photo. Analyse the stonemasonry. Discuss with your neighbour if this headstone "speaks" to you.

Headstone in an old Scottish graveyard